*Douglas Hyde*

## THE STONE OF TRUTH

Here are sixteen 'legends of saints and sinners', folk-stories mostly collected by Hyde from native speakers and translated by him. Some of these stories obviously come from continental sources; others are of a purely native invention; but all are typically Irish in their dovetailing of pagan and Christian elements.

Born in 1860, Douglas Hyde began to learn Irish at the age of fourteen. In 1893 he was present at the foundation of the Gaelic League and served as its first president. As professor of modern Irish at the National University, he devoted his life to the restoration of the Irish language and culture. In 1938 he was chosen to be the first president of independent Ireland. His numerous books and translations of Irish literature and folklore were probably the most influential single force behind the Irish literary renaissance. He died in 1949.

*Beside the Fire* and *The Love Songs of Connacht* are other Hyde books of folklore published by Irish Academic Press.

# THE STONE OF TRUTH
## and other Irish folk tales

*collected and translated from the Irish*

*by*

DOUGLAS HYDE

ROWMAN AND LITTLEFIELD
TOTOWA, NEW JERSEY

This selection by Gerard O'Flaherty was made from *Legends of Saints and Sinners* (Dublin 1915). Published by Irish Academic Press Limited, 3 Serpentine Avenue, Dublin 4, it was printed by Billing and Sons Limited, Guildford, England.

©Douglas Hyde Estate 1979

First published in the United States 1979. By Rowman and Littlefield, Totowa, N.J.

ISBN 0-8476-6232-2

PRINTED IN GREAT BRITAIN

## CONTENTS

| | |
|---|---|
| St Patrick and Crom Dubh | 9 |
| Knock Mulruana | 15 |
| The Stone of Truth | 21 |
| The Adventures of Leithin | 26 |
| Oscar of the Flail | 38 |
| The Priest who went to do Penance | 40 |
| The Friars of Urlaur | 48 |
| Shaun the Tinker | 56 |
| The Student who left College | 63 |
| The Old Woman of Beare | 68 |
| Friar Brian | 75 |
| St Patrick and his Garron | 77 |
| Teig O'Kane and the Corpse | 85 |
| The Buideach, the Tinker and the Black Donkey | 102 |
| God spare your health | 112 |
| St Peter | 114 |
| Mary's Well | 121 |

# ST. PATRICK AND CROM DUBH

BEFORE St. Patrick came to Ireland there lived a chieftain in the Lower Country[1] in Co. Mayo, and his name was Crom Dubh. Crom Dubh lived beside the sea in a place which they now call Dún Patrick, or Downpatrick, and the name which the site of his house is called by is Dún Briste, or Broken Fort. My story will tell why it was called Dún Briste.

It was well and it was not ill, brother of my heart! Crom Dubh was one of the worst men that could be found, but as he was a chieftain over the people of that country he had everything his own way; and that was the bad way, for he was an evil-intentioned, virulent, cynical,[2] obstinate man, with desire to be avenged on every one who did not please him. He had two sons, Téideach and Clonnach, and there is a big hollow going in under the road at Gleann Lasaire, and the name of this hollow in Poll a' Téidigh or Téideach's hole, for it got its name from Crom Dubh's son, and the name of this hole is on the mouth of [*i.e.*, used by] English-speaking people, though they do not know the meaning of it. Nobody knows how far this hole is going back under the glen, but it is said by the old Irish speakers that Téideach used to go every day in his little floating curragh into this hole under the glen, and that this is the reason it was called Téideach's Hole.

It was well, my dear. To continue the story, Crom

---

[1] Lower means "northern." It means round the Lagan, Creevagh and Ballycastle.
[2] Literally "doggish." The meaning is rather "snarling" or "fierce" than cynical.

Dubh's two sons were worse than himself, and that leaves them bad enough! Crom Dubh had two hounds of dogs and their names were Coinn Iotair and Saidhthe Suaraighe,[1] and if ever there were [wicked] mastiffs these two dogs were they. He had them tied to the two jaws of the door, in order to loose them and set them to attack people according as they might come that way; and, to go further, he had a big fire kindled on the brink of the cliff so that any one who might escape from the hounds he might throw into the fire; and to make a long story short, the fame of Crom Dubh and his two sons, and his two mastiffs, went far and wide, for their evil-doing; and the people were so terrified at his name, not to speak of himself, that they used to hide their faces in their bosoms when they used to hear it mentioned in their ears, and the people were so much afraid of him that if they heard the bark of a dog they would go hiding in the dwellings that they had underground, to take refuge in, to defend themselves from Crom Dubh and his mastiffs.

It is said that there was a linnaun shee[2] or fairy sweetheart walking with Crom Dubh, and giving him knowledge according as he used to require it. In place of his inclining to what was good as he was growing in age, the way he went on was to be growing in badness every day, and the wind was not quicker than he, for he was as nimble as a March hare. When he used to go out about the country he used to send his two sons and his two mastiffs before him, and they announcing to the people according as they proceeded, that Crom Dubh was coming to collect his standing rent, and bidding them to have it ready for him. Crom Dubh used to come after them, and his trickster (?) along with him, and he drawing after him a

---

[1] Pronounced like "Cunn eetir" and "sy-ha soory"—hound of rage and bitch of wickedness?

[2] Linnaun shee, a fairy sweetheart; in Irish spelt "leannán sidhe."

sort of yoke like a wheelless sliding car, and according as he used to get his standing-rent it used to be thrown into the car, and every one had to pay according to his ability. Anyone who would refuse, he used to be brought next day before Crom Dubh, as he sat beside the fire, and Crom used to pass judgment upon him, and after the judgment the man used to be thrown into the fire. Many a plan and scheme were hatched against Crom Dubh to put him out of the world, but he overcame them all, for he had too much wizardry from the [fairy] sweetheart.

Crom Dubh was continuing his evil deeds for many years, and according as the story about him remains living and told from person to person, they say that he was a native of hell in the skin of a biped, and through the horror that the people of the country had for him they would have given all that ever they saw if only Crom Dubh and his company could have been put-an-end-to ; but there was no help for them in that, since he and his company had the power, and they had to endure bitter persecution for years, and for many years, and every year it was getting worse ; and they without any hope of relief because they had no knowledge of God or Mary or of anything else which concerned heaven. For that reason they could not put trust in any person beyond Crom Dubh, because they thought, bad as he was, that it was he who was giving them the light of the day, the darkness of the night, and the change of seasons.

It was well, brother of my heart. During this time St. Patrick was going throughout Ireland, working diligently and baptizing many people. On he went until he came to Fo-choill or Foghill ; and at that time and for long afterwards there were nothing but woods that grew in that place, but there is neither branch nor tree there now. However, to pursue the story, St. Patrick began explaining to the Pagans about the light and glory of the heavens. Some of them gave ear to him, but the most of them paid him no attention. After he had taken all those who listened to him to the place which was called the Well of the Branch to baptize them, and when he had them baptized, the people called the well Tobar Phadraig, or Patrick's Well, and that is there ever since.

When these Pagans got the seal of Christ on their forehead, and knowledge of the Holy Trinity, they began telling St. Patrick about the doings of Crom Dubh and his evil ways, and they besought him if he had any power from the All-mighty Father to chastise Crom Dubh, rightly or wrongly, or to give him the Christian faith if it were possible.

It was well, brother, St. Patrick passed on over through Tráigh Leacan, up Béal Trághadh, down Craobhach, and down under the Logán, the name that was on Crom Dubh's place before St. Patrick came. When St. Patrick reached the Logán, which is near the present Ballycastle, he was within a quarter of a mile of Crom Dubh's house, and at the same time Crom Dubh and Téideach his son were trying a bout of wrestling with one another, while Saidhthe Suaraighe was stretched out on the ground from ear to tail. With the squeezing they were giving one another they never observed St. Patrick making for them until Saidhthe Suaraighe put a howling bark out of her, and with that the pair looked behind them and they saw St. Patrick and his defensive company with him, making for them; and in the twinkling of an eye the two rushed forward, clapping their hands and setting Saidhthe Suaraighe at them and encouraging her.

With that Téideach put his fore finger into his mouth and let a whistle calling for Coinn Iotair, for she was at that same time hunting with Clonnach on the top of Glen Lasaire, and Glen Lasaire is nearly two miles from Dun Phadraig, but she was not as long as while you'd be saying

De' raisias [Deo Gratias] coming from Glen Lasaire when she heard the sound of the whistle. They urged the two bitches against St. Patrick, and at the same time they did not know what sort of man St. Patrick was or where he came from.

The two bitches made for him and coals of fire out of their mouths, and a blue venomous light burning in their eyes, with the dint of venom and wickedness, but just as they were going to seize St. Patrick he cut [marked] a ring round about him with the crozier which he had in his hand, and before the dogs reached the verge of the ring St. Patrick spoke as follows :—

> A lock on thy claws, a lock on thy tooth,
> A lock on Coinn Iotair of the fury.
> A lock on the son and on the daughter of Saidhthe Suaraighe.
> A lock quickly, quickly on you.

Before St. Patrick began to utter these words there was a froth of foam round their mouths, and their hair was standing up as strong as harrow-pins with their fury, but after this as they came nearer to St. Patrick they began to lay down their ears and wag their tails. And when Crom Dubh saw that, he had like to faint, because he knew when they laid down their ears that they would not do any hurt to him they were attacking. The moment they reached St. Patrick they began jumping up upon him and making friendly with him. They licked both his feet from the top of his great toe[1] to the butt of his ankle, and that affection [thus manifesting itself] is amongst dogs from that day to this. St. Patrick began to stroke them with his hand and he went on making towards Crom Dubh, with the dogs walking at his heels. Crom Dubh ran until he came to the fire and he stood up beside the fire, so that he might throw St. Patrick

---

[1] Rather "the space between the toes."

into it when he should come as far as it. But as St. Patrick knew the strength of the fire beforehand he lifted a stone in his hand, signed the sign of the cross on the stone, and flung the stone so as to throw it into the middle of the flames, and on the moment the fire went down to the lowest depths of the ground, in such a way that the hole is there yet to be seen, from that day to this, and it is called Poll na Sean-tuine, the hole of the old fire (?), and when the tide fills, the water comes in to the bottom of the hole, and it would draw " deaf cows out of woods "—the noise that comes out of the hole when the tide is coming in.

It was well, company [1] of the world; when Crom Dubh saw that the fire had departed out of sight, and that the dogs had failed him and given him no help (a thing they had **never done before**), he himself and Téideach struck out like a blast of March wind until they reached the house, and St. Patrick came after them. They had not far to go, for the fire was near the house. When St. Patrick approached it he began to talk aloud with Crom Dubh, and he did his best to change him to a good state of grace, but it failed him to put the seal of Christ on his forehead, for he would not give any ear to St. Patrick's words.

Now there was no trick of deviltry, druidism, witchcraft, or black art in his heart, which he did not work for all he was able, trying to gain the victory over St. Patrick, but it was all no use for him, for the words of God were more powerful than the deviltry of the fairy] sweetheart.

With the dint of the fury that was on Crom Dubh and on Téideach his son, they began snapping and grinding their teeth, and so outrageous was their fury that St. Patrick gave a blow of his crozier to the cliff under the

---

[1] A variant of " it was well, my dear."

base of the gable of the house, and he separated that much of the cliff from the cliffs on the mainland, and that is to be seen there to-day just as well as the first day, and that is the cliff that is called Dún Briste or Broken Fort.

To pursue the story. All that much of the cliff is a good many yards out in the sea from the cliff on the mainland, so Crom Dubh and his son had to remain there until the midges and the scaldcrows had eaten the flesh off their bones. And that is the death that Crom Dubh got, and that is the second man that midges ate, and our ancient shanachies say that the first man that midges ate was Judas after he had hanged himself; and that is the cause why the bite of the midges is so sharp as it is.

To pursue the story still further. When Clonnach saw what had happened to his father he took fright, and he was terrified of St. Patrick, and he began burning the mountain until he had all that side of the land set on fire. So violently did the mountains take fire on each side of him that himself could not escape, and they say that he himself was burned to a lump amongst them.

St. Patrick returned back to Fochoill and round through Baile na Pairce, the Town of the Field, and Bein Buidhe, the Yellow Ben, and back to Clochar. The people gathered in multitudes from every side doing honourable homage to St. Patrick, and the pride of the world on them that an end had been made of Crom Dubh.

There was a well near and handy, and he brought the great multitude round about the well, and he never left mother's son or man's daughter without setting on their faces the wave of baptism and the seal of Christ on their foreheads. They washed and scoured the walls of the well, and all round about it, and they got forked branches and limbs of trees and bound white and blue ribbons on them, and set them round about the well, and every one of them bowed down on his knees saying their prayers of thankfulness to God, and as an entertainment for St. Patrick on account of his having put an end to the sway of Crom Dubh.

After making an end of offering up their prayers every man of them drank three sups of water out of the well, and there is not a year from that out that the people used not to make a *turus* or pilgrimage to the well, on the anniversary of that day; and that day is the last Sunday of the seventh month, and the name the Irish speakers call the month by in that place is the month of Lughnas [August] and the name of the Sunday is Crom Dubh's Sunday, but, the name that the English speakers call the Sunday by, is Garland Sunday. There is never a year from that to this that there does not be a meeting in Cill Chuimin, for that is the place where the well is. They come far and near to make a pilgrimage to the well; and a number of other people go there too, to amuse themselves and drink and spend. And I believe that the most of that rakish lot go there making a mock of the Christian Irish-speakers who are offering up their prayers to their holy patron Patrick, high head of their religion.

Cuimin's well is the name of this well, for its name was changed during the time of Saint Cuimin on account of all the miraculous things he did there, and he is buried within a perch of the well in Cill Chuimin.

There does be a gathering on the same Sunday at Dún Padraig or Downpatrick at the well which is called Tobar Brighde or Briget's Well beside Cill Brighde, and close to Dún Briste; but, love of my heart, since the English jargon began a short time ago in that place the old Christian custom of the Christians is almost utterly gone off.

There now ye have it as I got it, and if ye don't like it add to it your complaints.[1]

---

[1] Apparently tell it with your complaint added to it.

# KNOCK MULRUANA

On this side of Glen Domhain, there is a little hill whose name is Mulroney's Hill, and this is the reason why it was given that name.

In old times there was a man living in a little house on the side of the hill, and Mulruana was his name. He was a pious holy man, and hated the world's vanities so much that he became a hermit, and he was always alone in that house, without anyone in his neighbourhood. He used to be always praying and subduing himself. He used to drink nothing but water, and used to eat nothing but berries and the wild roots which he used to get in the mountains and throughout the glens. His fame and reputation were going through the country for the holy earnest life that he was living.

However, great jealousy seized the Adversary at the piety of this man, and he sent many evil spirits to put temptations on him. But on account of all his prayers and piety it failed those evil-spirits to get the victory over him, so that they all returned back to hell with the report of the steadfastness and loyalty of Mulruana in the service of God.

Then great anger seized Satan, so that he sent further demons, each more powerful than the other, to put temptation on Mulruana. Not one of them succeeded in even coming near the hut of the holy man. Nor did it fare any better with them whenever he came outside, for he used always to be attentive to his prayers and ever musing on holy things. Then every evil-spirit of them used to go back to hell and used to tell the devil that there was no use contending with Mulruana, for that God himself and His angels were keeping him and giving him help.

That account made Satan mad entirely, so that he determined at last to go himself, hoping to destroy Mulruana, and to draw him out of the proper path. Accordingly he came one evening at nightfall, in the guise of a young woman, and asked the good man for lodging. Mulruana rudely refused the pretended woman, and banished her away from his door, although he felt a compassion for her because the night was wet and stormy, and he thought that the girl was without house and shelter from the rain and cold. But what the woman did was to go round to the back of the house and play music, and it was the sweetest and most melancholy music that man ever heard.

Because Mulruana had had a pity for the poor girl at the first, he listened now to her music, and took great delight in it, and had much joy of it, but he did not allow her into his hut. At the hour of midnight the devil went back to hell, but he had a shrewd notion that he had won the game and that he had caught the holy man. Mulruana had quiet during the remainder of the night, but instead of continuing at his prayers, as was his custom, he spent the end of the night, almost till the dawn of day, thinking of the beauty of the girl and of the sweetness of her music

The day after that the devil came at the fall of night in the same likeness, and again asked lodging of Mulruana. Mulruana refused that, although he did not like to do it, but he remembered the vow he had made never to let a woman or a girl into his hut. The pretended woman went round to the back of the house, and she was playing music that was like fairy music until it was twelve o'clock, when she had to go away with herself to hell. The man inside was listening to the playing and taking great delight in it, and when she ceased there came over him melancholy and trouble of mind. He never slept a wink that night, and he never said a word of his prayers either, but eagerly thinking[1] of the young woman, and his heart going astray with the beauty of her form and the sweetness of her voice.

On the morning of the next day Mulruana rose from his bed, and it is likely that it was the whisper of an angel he heard, because he remembered that it was not right for him to pay such heed to a girl and to forget his prayers. He bowed his knees and began to pray strongly and earnestly, and made a firm resolve that he would not think more about the girl, and that he would not listen to her music. But, after all, he did not succeed in obtaining a complete victory over his thoughts concerning the young woman, and consequently he was between two notions until the evening came.

When the night was well dark the Adversary came again in the shape of the girl, and she even more beautiful and more lovely than she was before, and asked the man for a night's lodging. He remembered his vow and the resolve he had made that day in the morning, and he refused her, and threatened her that she should not come again to trouble him, and he drove her away with rough sharp words, and with a stern, churlish countenance, as though there were a great anger on him. He went into his hut and the girl remained near the hut outside, and she weeping and lamenting and shedding tears.

When Mulruana saw the girl weeping and keening piteously he conceived a great pity for her, and compassion for her came to him, and desire, and he did not free his heart from those evil inclinations, since he had

---

[1] This idiom, borrowed from the Irish, is very common in Anglo-Irish. It is not governed by the rules of English grammar.

not made his prayers on that day with a heart as pure as had been his wont, and he listened willingly and gladly. It was not long until he came out, himself, in spite of his vow and his good resolutions, and invited the pretended woman to come into his hut. Small delay she made in going in!

It was then the King of Grace took pity at this man being lost without giving him time to amend himself, since he had ever been truly pious, diligent, humane, well disposed and of good works, until this great temptation came over him. For that reason God sent an angel to him with a message to ask him to repent. The angel came to Mulruana's house and went inside. Then the devil leapt to his feet, uttered a fearful screech, changed his colour, his shape, and his appearance. His own devilish form and demoniac appearance came upon him. He turned away from the angel like a person blinded with a great shining or blaze of light, and went out of the hut.

His senses nearly departed from Mulruana with the terror that overcame him. When he came to himself again the angel made clear to him how great was the sin to which he had given way, and how God had sent him to him to ask him to repent. But Mulruana never believed a word he said. He knew that it was the devil who had been in his company in the guise of a young woman. He remembered the sin to which he had consented, so that he considered himself to be so guilty that it would be impossible for him ever to obtain forgiveness from God. He thought that it was deceiving him the angel was, when he spoke of repentance and forgiveness. The angel was patient with him and spoke gently. He told him of the love and friendship of God and how He would never refuse forgiveness to the truly penitent, no matter how heavy his share of sins. Mulruana did not listen to him, but a drowning-man's-cry issued out of his mouth always, that he was lost, and he ever-cursing God, the devil and himself. The angel never ceased, but entreating and beseeching him to turn to God and make repentance—but it was no use for him. Mulruana was as hard and as stubborn as he was before, all the time taking great oaths and blaspheming God.

All the time the angel was speaking he had the appearance of a burning candle in his hand. At long last, when the candle was burnt all but about an inch, a gloom fell over the countenance of the angel and he stood out from Mulruana, and threatened him, and told him that his term of grace was almost expired, and, said he, unless you make repentance before this inch of candle is burnt away, God will grant you no more respite, and you will be damned for ever.

Then there came silence on Mulruana for a while, as though he were about to follow the advice of the angel. But then on the spot he thought of the sin that he had done. On that, despair seized him, and the answer he gave the angel was, " as I have burned the candle I'll burn the inch." Then the angel spoke to him with a loud and terrible voice, announcing to him that he was now indeed accursed of God, and, said he, " thou shalt die to-morrow of thirst." Mulruana answered him with no submission, and said, " O lying angel, I know now that you are deceiving me. It is impossible that I should die of thirst in this place, and so much water round about me. There is, outside there, a well of spring water that was never dry, and there is a stream beside the gable of the house which would turn the wheel of a great mill no matter how dry the summer day, and down there is Loch Beithe on which a fleet of ships might float. It is a great folly for you to say that anybody could die of thirst in this place." But the angel departed from him without an answer.

Mulruana went to lie down after that, but, if he did, he never slept a wink through great trouble of spirit. Next morning, on his rising early, the sharpest thirst that man ever felt came upon him. He leapt out of his bed and went to the stoap [pail] for water, but there was not a drop in it. Out with him then to the well, but he did not find a drop there either. He turned on his foot towards the stream that was beside the house, but it was dry before him down to the gravel. The banks and the pebbles in the middle of it were as dry as though they had never seen a drop of water for a year. Mulruana remembered then the prophecy of the angel and he started. A quaking of terror came upon him, and his thirst was growing every moment. He went running at full speed to Loch Beithe, but when he came to the brink of the lake he uttered one awful cry and fell in a heap on the ground. Loch Beithe too was dry before him

That is how a cowherd found him the next day, lying on the brink of the lake, his eyes starting out of his head, his tongue stretched out of his throat, and a lump of white froth round his mouth. His awful appearance was such that fear would not let the people go near him to bury him, and his body was left there until birds of prey and wild dogs took it away with them.

That is how it happened Mulruana as a consequence of his sin, his impenitence, and his despair, and that is the reason why it is not right for any one to use the old saying, " As I've burnt the candle I'll burn the inch," and yonder is " Cnoc Mhaoilruanadha," Mulruana's Hill, as a witness to the truth of this story

# THE STONE OF TRUTH OR THE MERCHANT OF THE SEVEN BAGS

THERE was a man in it, hundreds and hundreds of years ago, whose name was Páidin[1] O Ciarbháin [Keerwaun, or Kerwin] and he was living close to Cong in West Connacht. Páidin was a strange man; he did not believe in God or in anything about him. It's often the priest thought to bring him to Mass, but it was no use for him, for Páidin would not take the advice of priest or bishop. He believed that man was like the beast, and he believed that when man died there was no more about him.

Páidin lived an evil life; he used to be going from house to house by day, and stealing in the night.

Now, at the time that St. Patrick was in West Connacht seeking to make Christians of the Pagans, he went down one day upon his knees, on a great flag stone, to utter prayers, and he left after him a great virtue in the same stone, for anybody who might speak above that stone, it was necessary for him to tell the clear truth, he could not tell a lie, and for that reason the people gave the name to that flag of the Stone of Truth

Páidin used always to have a great fear of this stone, and it's often he intended to steal it. One night when he found an opportunity he hoisted the stone on his back, took it away with him, and threw it down into a great valley between two hills, seven miles from the place where it used to be, and the rogue thought that he was all right; but the stone was back in its old place that same night without his knowing.

---

[1] Pronounced "Paudyeen."

Another night after that he stole the geese of the parish priest, and as the people doubted him, they said that they would bring him to the Stone of Truth. Páidin was laughing in his own mind, for he knew that he had the stone stolen ; but great was the surprise that was on him when he saw the stone before him in its own place. When he was put above the stone he was obliged to tell that he had stolen the geese, and he got a great beating from the priest. He made a firm resolution then that if he got an opportunity at the stone again, he would put it in a place that it would never come out of.

A couple of nights after that he got his opportunity again, and stole the stone a second time. He threw it down into a great deep hole, and he went home rejoicing in himself. But he did not go a quarter of a mile from the place until he heard a great noise coming after him. He looked behind him and he saw a lot of little people, and they dressed in clothes as white as snow. There came such fear over Páidin that he was not able to walk one step, until the little people came up with him, and they carrying the Stone of Truth with them. A man of them spoke to him and said : " O accursed Páidin, carry this stone back to the place where you got it, or you shall pay dearly for it."

" I will and welcome," said Páidin.

They put the stone upon his back and they returned the road on which they had come. But as the devil was putting temptation upon Páidin, he went and threw the stone into a hole that was deeper than the first hole, a hole which the people made to go hiding in when the war would be coming. The stone remained in that hole for more than seven years, and no one knew where it was but Páidin only.

At the end of that time Páidin was going by the side of the churchyard, when he looked up at a cross that was standing there, and he fell into a faint. When he came to himself, there was a man before him and he clothed as white as the snow. He spoke to him and said: "O accursed Páidin, you are guilty of the seven deadly sins, and unless you do penance you shall go to hell. I am an angel from God, and I will put a penance on you. I will put seven bags upon you and you must carry them for one and twenty years. After that time go before the great cross that shall be in the town of Cong, and say three times, ' My soul to God and Mary,' spend a pious life until then, and you will go to heaven. Go to the priest now, if you are obedient (and ready) to receive my counsel."

" I am obedient," said Páidin, " but the people will be making a mock of me."

" Never mind the mock, it won't last long," said the angel.

After this conversation a deep sleep fell upon Páidin, and when he awoke there were seven bags upon him, and the angel was gone away. There were two bags on his right side, two bags on his left side, and three others on his back, and they were stuck so fast upon him that he thought that it was growing on him they were. They were the colour of his own skin, and there was skin on them. Next day when Páidin went among the people he put wonder on them, and they called him the Merchant of the Seven Bags, and that name stuck to him until he died.

Páidin began a new life now. He went to the priest, and he showed him the seven bags that were on him, and he told him the reason that they were put on him. The priest gave him good advice and a great coat to cover the seven bags with; and after that Páidin used to be going from house to house and from village to village asking alms, and there used never be a Sunday or holiday that he would not be at Mass, and there used to be a welcome before him in every place.

About seven years after that Páidin was going by the side of the hole into which he had thrown the Stone of Truth. He came to the brink of the hole, went down on his two knees and asked God to send him up the stone. When his prayer was ended he saw the stone coming up, and hundreds of white doves round about it. The stone was rising and ever rising until it came into Páidin's presence on the ground, and then the doves went back again. The next day he went to the priest and told him everything about the Stone of Truth, and the way it came up out of the hole. " I will go with you," said the priest, " until I see this great wonder." The priest went with him to the hole and he saw the Stone of Truth. And he saw another thing which put great wonder on him ; thousands and thousands of doves flying round about the mouth of the hole, going down into it and coming up again. The priest called the place Poll na gColum or the Dove's Hole, and that name is on it until the present day. The blessed stone was brought into Cong, and it was not long until a grand cross was erected over it, and from that day to this people come from every place to look at the Doves' Hole, and the old people believed that they were St. Patrick's angels who were in those doves.

The Stone of Truth was for years after that in Cong, and it is certain that it did great good, for it kept many people from committing crimes. But it was stolen at last, and there is no account of it from that out.

Páidin lived until he was four score years of age, and bore his share of penance piously. When the one and twenty years that the angel gave him were finished, and he carrying the seven bags throughout that time, there came a messenger in a dream to say to him that his life in this world was finished, and that he must go the next day before the Cross of Cong and give himself up to God and Mary. Early in the morning he went to the priest and told him the summons he had got in the night. People say that the priest did not believe him, but at all events he told Páidin to do as the messenger had bidden him.

Páidin departed, and left his blessing with his neighbours and relations, and when the clock was striking twelve, and the people saying the Angelical Salutation, Páidin came before the cross and said three times, " My soul to God and to Mary," and on the spot he fell dead.

That cross was in the town of Cong for years. A bishop, one of the O'Duffy's, went to Rome, and he got a bit of the true Cross and put it into the Cross of Cong. It was there until the foreigners came and threw it to the ground. The Cross of Cong is still in Ireland, and the people have an idea that it will yet be raised up in the town of Cong with the help of God.

# THE ADVENTURES OF LÉITHIN

A GENTLE, noble, renowned patron there was of a time in the land of Ireland, whose exact name was Ciaran of Cluan.[1] A good faith had he in the mighty Lord.

One day Ciaran bade his clerics to go look for thatch for his church, on a Saturday of all days,[2] and those to whom he spake were Sailmin, son of Beogan, and Maolan, son of Naoi, for men submissive to God were they twain, so far as their utmost diligence went, and many miracles were performed for Maolan, as Ciaran said in the stanza,

> Maolan, son of Naoi the cleric,
> His right hand be for our benison
> If the son of Naoi desired it
> To work miracles like every saint.

And, moreover, Sailmin, son of Beogan, he was the same man of whom, for wisdom, for piety, and for religion, Ciaran spake the stanza,

> Sailmin melodious, son of Beogan.
> A faith godlike and firm.
> No blemish is in his body.
> His soul is an angel.

He was the seventh son of the sons of Beogan of Burren,[3] and those men were the seven psalmists of Ciaran, so that from them are the "Youth's Cross" on the Shannon, and the [other] "Youth's Cross" on the high road to Clonmacnoise [named].

Howsoever the clerics fared forth alongside the Shannon, until they reached Cluain Doimh. There they cut the full of their little curragh of white-bottomed

---

[1] *i.e.*, Clonmacnoise.  [2] Literally "especially."  [3] In West Clare.

green-topped rushes. But [before they had done] they heard the voice of the clerics' bell at the time of vespers on Sunday, so they said that they would not leave that place until the day should rise on them on Monday, and they spake the lay as follows :

> The voice of a bell I heard in Cluan[1]
> On Sunday night defeating us,
> I shall not depart since that has been heard,
> Until Monday, after the Sunday.
>
> On Sunday did God shape-out Heaven,
> On that day was the King of the apostles born ;
> On Sunday was born Mary
> Mother of the King of Mercy.
>
> On Sunday, I say it,
> Was born victorious John Baptist.
> By the hand of God in the stream in the East
> Was he baptised on Sunday.
>
> On Sunday, moreover, it is a true thing,
> The Son of God took the captivity out of hell.
> On a Sunday after the battle . . . ?
> Shall God deliver the judgment of the last day.
>
> On a Sunday night, we think it melodious,
> The voice of the cleric I hear,
> The voice I hear of a bell
> On Drum Diobraid above the pool.
>
> The voice of the bell I hear
> Making me to postpone-return
> The voice of the bell I hear
> Bringing me to Cluan.
>
> By thy hand O youth,
> And by the King who created thee,
> My heart thinks it delightful
> The bell and the voice.

Howbeit the clerics abode that night [where they were] for the love of the King of Sunday. Now there occurred, that night, a frost and a prolonged snow and a rigour of cold, and there arose wind and tempest in the elements for their skaith, without as much as a bothy or a lean-to of a bed or a fire for them, and surely were it not for the mercy of God protecting them round about, it was

---

[1] *i.e.*, Clonmacnoise.

not in the mind of either of them that he should be alive on the morrow after that night, with all they experienced of oppression and terror from the great tempest of that wild-weather, so that they never remembered their acts of piety or to say or sing a prayer (?) Nor could they sleep or rest, for their senses were turned to foolishness, for they had never seen the like or the equal of that storm, and of the bad weather of that night, for the venom of its cold and moreover for the bitterness of the morning [which followed it]. And as they were there on the morning of the next day they heard a gentle, low, lamentable, woe-begone conversation of grief above their heads on high, on a tall, wide-extended cliff. And [the meaning] was revealed to them through the virtue of their holiness, and although much evil and anxiety had they suffered, [still] they paid attention to the conversation and observed it. And they between whom the conversation was, were these, namely an eagle who was called Léithín[1] and a bird of her birds[2] in dialogue with her, piteously and complainingly lamenting their cold-state, pitifully, sadly, grievously; and said the bird to the eagle:

"Léithin," said he, "do you ever remember the like of this morning or of last night to have come within thy knowledge before?"

"I do not remember," said Léithin. "that I ever heard or saw the like or the equal of them, since the world was created, and do you yourself remember, or did you ever hear of such [weather]?" said the eagle to the bird.

"There are people who do remember," said the bird.

"Who are they?" said the eagle.

"Dubhchosach, the Black-footed one of Binn Gulban,[3]

---

[1] Apparently "the little grey one," from "liath"-grey; pronounced "Lay-heen." I have made her feminine and called her "she" in the translation, but the Irish makes her masculine.

[2] i.e., one of its own young eagles, or nestlings.

[3] Now Ben Bulben in Co. Sligo.

that is the vast-sized stag of the deluge,[1] who is at Binn Gulban ; and he is the hero of oldest memory of all those of his generation (?) in Ireland.

" Confusion on thee and skaith ! surely thou knowest not that ; and now although that stag be far away from me I shall go to see him, to find if I may get any knowledge from him ! "

Therewith Léithin went off lightly, yet was she scarcely able to rise up on high with the strength of the bad weather, and no more could she go low with the cold of the . . . ? and with the great abundance of the water, and, though it was difficult for her, she progressed lightly and lowflying, and no one living could reveal or make known all that she met of evil and of misery going to Ben Gulban looking for the Blackfoot. And she found the smallheaded swift-footed stag scratching himself against a bare oak rampike. And Léithin descended on a corner of the rampike beside him. And she saluted the stag in his own language and asks him was he the Blackfoot. The stag said that he was, and Léithin spoke the lay :

> Well for you O Blackfoot,
>   On Ben Gulban high,
> Many moors and marshes,
>   Leap you lightly by.
>
> Hounds no more shall hunt you
>   Since the Fenians fell,
> Feeding now untroubled
>   On from glen to glen.
>
> Tell me stag high-headed,
>   Saw you ever fall
> Such a night and morning ?
>   You remember all.
>
> [THE STAG ANSWERS.]
> I will give you answer
>   Léithin wise and gray,
> Such a night and morning
>   Never came my way.

---

[1] *i.e.*, " As old as the deluge."

"Tell me, Blackfoot," said Léithin, "what is thy age?"

"I shall tell thee," said the Blackfoot. "I remember this oak here when it was a little sapling, and I was born at the foot of the oak sapling, and I was reared upon that couch [of moss at its foot] until I was a mighty-great stag, and I loved this abode [ever], through my having been reared here. And the oak grew after that till it was a giant oak (?) and I used to come and constantly scratch myself against it every evening after my journeyings and goings [during the day] and I used [always] to remain beside it in such wise till the next morning, and if I had to make a journey or were hotly hunted I used to reach the same tree, so that we grew up with one another, until I became a mighty-great stag, and this tree became the bare withered rampike which you see, so that it is now only a big ruined shapeless-stump without blossom or fruit or foliage to-day, its period and life being spent. Now I have let a long period of years[1] go by me, yet I never saw and never heard tell-of, in all that time, the like of last night."

Léithin departs [to return] to his birds after that, and on his reaching home the other[2] bird spoke to him, "have you found out what you went to inquire about?"

"I have not," said Léithin, and she began to revile the bird for all the cold and hardships she had endured, but at last she said, "who do you think again would know this thing for me?" said Léithin.

"I know that," said the bird, "Dubhgoire the Black caller of Clonfert[3] of Berachan."

"Well then I shall go seek him."

---

[1] Or, "a cargo of five hundred years."
[2] Literally "second."
[3] Perhaps "Cluansost." There is no Berachan in Clonfert in the martyrologies.

And although that was far away from her, yet she proceeded until she reached Clonfert of St. Berachan, and she was observing the birds until they had finished their feeding [and were returning home], and then Léithin saw one splendid bird beautifully-topped, victorious-looking, of the size of a blackbird, but of the brightness of a swan, and as soon as it came into its presence Léithin asks it whether it were Dubhgoire. It said that it was. It was a marvel [to Léithin] when it said that it was, namely that the blackbird should be white, and Léithin spake the lay.

"How is that O Dubhgoire, sweet is thy warbling, often hast thou paid thy calls throughout the blue-leaved forest.

" In Clonfert of the bright streams and by the full plain of the Liffey, and from the plain of the Liffey coming from the east to Kildare behind it.

"From that thou departest to thy nest in the Cill which Brigit blessed. Short was it for thee to overleap every hedge till thou camest to the townland in which Berachan was.

" O Dubhgoire tell to me—and to count up all thy life—the like of yesterday morning, didst thou ever experience it, O Dubhgoire ? "

[DUBHGOIRE ANSWERS.]

"To me my full life was three hundred years before Berachan, the lifetime of Berachan I spent [added thereto], I was enduring in lasting happiness.

"Since the time that Lughaidh of the Blades was for a while in the sovereignty of all Ireland I never experienced by sea or by land such weather as that which Léithin mentions in his lay." [1]

---

[1] Literally, "I never got on sea or land a knowledge of that lay of Léithin's."

"Well, then, my own errand to thee," said Léithin, "is to enquire if thou didst ever experience, or remember to have seen or [to have heard] that there ever came such a morning as yesterday for badness."

"I do not remember that I ever saw such," said Dubhgoire, "or anything like it."

As for Léithin, she was sad and sorrowful, for those tidings did not help (?) her, and she proceeded on her way till she reached her nest and birds.

"What have you to tell us to-day?" said the bird.

"May you never have luck nor fortune," said Léithin. "I have no more news for you than I had when departing, except all my weariness from all the journeyings and wanderings which you contrive to get me to take, without my getting any profit or advantage out of you," and with that she gave a greedy venemous drive of her beak at the bird, so that she had like to have made a prey and flesh-torn spoil of it, with vexation at all the evil and misery she had experienced going to Kildare, so that the bird screeched out loudly and pitifully and miserably.

[A while] after that Léithin said, "It's a pity and a grief to me if any one in Ireland knows [that there ever came a night worse than that night] that I myself do not know of it."

"Well, then, indeed, there is one who knows," says the bird, "Goll of Easruaidh (*i.e.*, the Blind One of Assaroe) and another name of him is the Éigne[1] of Ath-Seannaigh (*i.e.*, the salmon of Ballyshannon), and it is certain that he knows about that, if any one in the world knows about it."

"It is hard for me to go the way you tell me," said Léithin, "yet should I like exceeding well to know about this thing."

Howsoever she set out, and she never came down until

---
[1] This is an old poetic word for a salmon.

she reached Assaroe of Mac Modhuirn, and she began observing and scrutinizing Assaroe until she saw the salmon feeding near the ford, and she saluted him and said, " Delightful is that O Goll, it is not with thee as with me, for our woes are not the same," and she spake the lay :

[LEITHIN SPEAKS.]

" Pleasant is that [life of thine] O Goll with success (?) many is the stream which thou hast adventured, not the same for thee and for us, if we were to relate our wanderings.

" It is to thee that I have come from my house, O Blind one of Assaroe, how far doth thy memory go back, or how far is thy age to be reckoned ? "

[THE SALMON ANSWERS.]

" As for my memory, that is a long one. It is not easy to reckon it. There is not on land or in bush a person like me—none like me but myself alone !

" I remember, it is not a clear-cut remembrance, the displacing showers of the Deluge, four women and four men, who remained after it in the world.

" I remember Patrick of the pens coming into the land of Ireland, and the Fir Bolg, manful the assembly, coming from Greece to take possession of it.

" Truly do I mind me of Fintan's coming into the country close to me. Four men were the crew of his ship, and an equal number of females.

" I remember gentle Partholan's taking the kingship over Ulster. I remember, a while before that, Glas, son of Aimbithe in Emania.

" I chanced to be one morning that was fair, on this river, O Léithin, I never experienced a morning like that, either before it or after it.

" I gave a leap into the air under the brow of my hard

rock [here], and before I came down into my house [of water] this pool was one flag of ice.

"The bird of prey[1] seized me above the land with a furious ungentle onslaught, and bore away my clear blue eye. To me it was not a pleasant world."

"Well now, my own object in coming to thee," said Léithin, "was to enquire of thee whether thou dost ever remember such a morning as was yesterday?"

"Indeed saw I such a morning," quoth Goll. "I remember the coming of the deluge, and I remember the coming of Partholan and of Fintan and the children of Neimhidh and the Fir Bolg and the Tuatha De Danann, and the Fomorians and the sons of Milesius and Patrick son of Alprunn, and I remember how Ireland threw off from her those troops, and I remember a morning that was worse than that morning, another morning not speaking of the great showers out of which the deluge fell. And the deluge left only four men and four women, namely, Noe, son of Laimhfhiadh and his wife, and Sem, Cam and Japhet, and their three wives, for in truth that was the crew of the ark, and neither [church] man nor canon reckon that God left undestroyed in the world but those four. However, wise men truly recount that God left another four keeping knowledge and tribal-descent and preserving universal genealogies, for God did not wish the histories of the people to fade, and so he left Fintan son of Laimhfhiadh towards the setting of the sun, south, keeping an account of the west of the world, and, moreover, Friomsa Fhurdhachta keeping the lordship of the north, and the prophet and the Easba? duly ordering [the history of the] south. And those are they who were alive outside of the ark, and I

---

[1] Literally "eagle," but this is a mistake, it was not an eagle.

remember all those people. And Léithin," said Goll, " I never saw the like of that morning for vemon except one other morning that was worse than the morning that you speak of, and worse than any morning that ever came before it. It was thus. One day I was in this pool and I saw a beautifully coloured butterfly with purple spots in the air over my head. I leapt to catch it, and before I came down the whole pool had become one flag of ice behind me, so that [when I fell back] it bore me up And then there came the bird of prey[1] to me, on his seeing me [in that condition], and he gave a greedy venemous assault on me and plucked the eye out of my head, and only for my weight he would have lifted me, and he threw the eye into the pool, and we both wrestled together until we broke the ice with the violence of the struggle, and with the [heat of the] great amount of crimson-red blood that was pouring from my eye, so that the ice was broken by that, so that with difficulty I got down into the pool [again], and that is how I lost my eye. And it is certain O Léithin," said Goll, " that that was by far the worst morning that I ever saw, and worse than this morning that thou speakest of."

Now as for the clerics, they took council with one another, and determined to await [the eagle's return] that they might know what she had to relate. However they experienced such hardships and anguish from the cold and misery of the night, and they could not [despite their resolution] endure to abide [the eagle's return]. So Maolan, the cleric, said, " I myself beseech the powerful Lord, and the chosen Trinity, that the eagle, Léithin, may come with the knowledge she receives to Clonmacnoise and tell it to Ciaran," [and therewith they themselves departed.]

---

[1] Literally "eagle." MSS. reads "fiolar"—" the eagle," which is evidently a mistake.

Now as for Goll [the salmon], he asked Léithin, after that, who was it that sent her in pursuit of that knowledge

"It was the second bird of my own birds."

"That is sad," said Goll, "for that bird is much older than thou or than I either, and that is the bird that picked my eye out of me, and if he had desired to make thee wise in these things it would have been easy for him. That bird," said he, "is the old Crow of Achill. And its talons have got blunted with old age, and since its vigour and energy and power of providing for itself have departed from it, its way of getting food is to go from one nest to another, smothering and killing every bird's young, and eating them, and so thou shalt never overtake thy own birds alive. And O beloved friend, best friend that I ever saw, if thou only succeedest in catching him alive on thy return, remember all the tricks he has played thee, and avenge thy birds and thy journeyings and thy wanderings upon him, and then too mind thee to avenge my eye."

Léithin bade farewell to Goll, and off she went the selfsame way she had come, in a mighty swift course, for she felt certain [now] that she would not overtake her birds alive in her nest. And good cause had she for that dread, for she only found the place of the nest, wanting its birds, they having been eaten by the Crow of Achill. So that all Léithin got as the result of her errand was the loss of her birds.

But the old Crow of Achill had departed after its despoiling [the nest], so that Léithin did not come upon it, neither did she know what way it had gone.

Another thing, too, Léithin had to go every Monday, owing to the cleric's prayer, to Clonmacnoise. There the eagle perched upon the great pinnacle of the round tower[1]

---

[1] Literally "Bell-house."

of Clonmacnoise, and revealed herself to the holy patron, namely Ciaran. And Ciaran asked her for her news. And Léithin said she was [not ?] more grieved at her wanderings and her loss than at that. Thereupon Ciaran said that he would give her the price and reward of her storytelling ; namely, every time that her adventures should be told, if it were stormy or excessive rain that was in it at the time of telling, it should be changed into fine sky and good weather.

And Léithin said that it was understood by her [all along] that it was not her birds or her nest she would receive from him ; and since that might not be, she was pleased that her journeyings and wanderings should not go for nothing.

And [thereupon] Léithin related her goings from the beginning to the end, just as we have told them above. So those are the adventures of Léithin. Thus far.

# OSCAR OF THE FLAIL

SAINT PATRICK came to Ireland, and Oisín met him in Elphin and he carrying stones.

> And whatever time it might be that he got the food,
> It would be long again till he would get the drink.

"Oisín," says he, " let me baptize you."

"Oh, what good would that do me?" says Oisín.

"Oisín," says St. Patrick, "unless you let me baptize you, you will go to hell where the rest of the Fenians are."

"If," says Oisín, " Diarmaid and Goll were alive for us, and the king that was over the Fenians, if they were to go to hell they would bring the devil and his forge up out of it on their back."

"Listen, O gray and senseless Oisín, think upon God, and bow your knee, and let me baptize you."

"Patrick," says Oisín, "for what did God damn all that of people?"

"For eating the apple of commandment," says St. Patrick.

"If I had known that your God was so narrow-sighted that he damned all that of people for one apple, we would have sent three horses and a mule carrying apples to God's heaven to Him."

"Listen, O gray and senseless Oisín, think upon God, and bow your knee, and let me baptize you.

Oisín fell into a faint, and the clergy thought that he had died. When he woke up out of it, "O Patrick, baptize me," says he—he saw something in his faint, he saw the thing that was before him. The spear was in St. Patrick's hand, and he thrust it into Oisín's foot purposely ; and the ground was red with his share of blood.

" Oh," says St. Patrick to Oisín, " you are greatly cut."

" Oh, isn't that for my baptism ? " says Oisín.

" I hope in God that you are saved," says St. Patrick, " you have undergone baptism and . . . . ?"

" Patrick," says Oisín, " would you not be able to take the Fenians out of hell "—he saw them there when he was in his sleep.

" I could not," says St. Patrick, " and any one who is in hell, it is impossible to bring him out of it."

" Patrick," says Oisín, " are you able to take me to the place where Finn and the Fenians of Erin are ? "

" I cannot," says St. Patrick.

> As much as the humming gnat
> Or a scintilla of the beam of the sun,
> Unknown to the great powerful king
> Shall not pass in beneath my shield.

" Can you give them relief from the pain ? " says Oisín.

St. Patrick then asked it as a petition from God to give them a relief from their pain, and he said to Oisín that they had found relief. This is the relief they got from God. Oscar got a flail, and he requested a fresh thong to be put into the flail, and there went a green rush as a thong into it, and he got the full of his palm of green sand, and he shook the sand on the ground, and as far as the sand reached the devils were not able to follow ; but if they were to come beyond the place where the sand was strewn, Oscar was able to follow *them*, and to beat them with the flail. Oscar and all the Fenians are on this side of the sand, and the devils are on the other side, for St. Patrick got it as a request from God that they should not be able to follow them where the sand was shaken,— and the thong that was in the flail never broke since !

# THE PRIEST WHO WENT TO DO PENANCE

There arose some little difference between three sons. A farmer's sons they were. One man of them said that he would leave home and go to an island (*i.e.*, emigrate). Another man of them became a priest, and the eldest brother remained at home.

The young priest never stopped until he went to Athlone to the college there, and he remained there for five years until his term had expired, and he was turned out a professed priest. He got himself ready, then, in the college, and said that he would go home to visit his father and mother.

He bound his books together in his bag, and then he faced for home. There was no mode of conveyance at that time; he had to walk. He walked all through the day until night was coming on. He saw a light at a distance from him. He went to it and found a gentleman's big house. He came into the yard and asked for lodgings until the morning. He got that from the gentleman and welcome, and the gentleman did not know what he would do for him, with the regard he had for him.

The priest was a fine handsome man, and the daughter of the gentleman took, as you would say, a fancy to him, when she was bringing his supper—and a fine supper it was he got. When they went to sleep then the young woman went into the room where the priest was. She began entreating him to give up the church and to marry herself. The gentleman had no daughter but herself, and she was to have the house and place, all of it, and she told that to the priest.

Says the priest, " don't tell me your mind," says he; " it's no good. I am wed already to Mary Mother, and I shall never have any other wife," says he. She gave him up then when she saw that it was no good for her, and she went away. There was a piece of gold plate in the house, and when the young priest fell asleep she came back again into his room, and she put the gold plate unbeknownst to him into his bag, and out she went again.

When he rose then, in the morning, he was getting himself ready to be going off again. It was a Friday, a fast day, that was in it, but she got a piece of meat and put it into his pocket, unbeknownst to him. Now he had both the meat and the gold plate in his bag, and off my poor man went, without any meal in the morning. When he had gone a couple of miles on his road, up she rose and told her father that the man that he had last night with him, " it was a bad man he was, that he stole the gold plate, and that he had meat in his pocket, going away of him, that she herself saw him eating it as he went the road that morning." Then the father got ready a horse and pursued him, and came up with him and got him taken and brought back again to his own house, and sent for the peelers.

" I thought," said he, " that it was an honest man you were, and it's a rogue you are," said he.

He was taken out then and given to the jury to be tried, and he was found guilty. The father took the gold plate out of the bag and showed it to the whole jury. He was sentenced to be hanged then. They said that any man who did a thing of that sort, he deserved nothing but to put his head in the noose[1] and hang him.

He was up on the stage then going to be hanged,

---

[1] Literally, " in the gallows."

when he asked leave to speak in the presence of the people. That was given him. He stood up, then, and he told all the people who he himself was, and where he was going and what he had done; how he was going home to his father and mother, and how he came into the gentleman's house. "I don't know that I did anything bad," said he, "but the daughter that this gentleman had, she came in to me, into the room, where I was asleep, and she asked me to leave the church and to marry herself, and I would not marry her, and no doubt it was she who put the gold plate and the fish into my bag," and he went down on his two knees then, and put up a petition to God to send them all light that it was not himself who was guilty.

"Oh, it was not fish that was in your bag at all but meat," said the daughter.

"It was meat perhaps that *you* put in it, but it was fish that I found in it," says the priest.

When the people heard that, they desired to bring the bag before them, and they found that it was fish in the place of meat that was in it. They gave judgment then to hang the young woman instead of the priest.

She was put up then in place of him to be hanged, and when she was up on the stage, going to be hanged, "Well, you devil," said she, "I'll have you, in heaven or on earth," and with that she was hanged.

The priest went away after that, drawing on home. When he came home he got, after a while, a chapel and a parish, and he was quiet and satisfied, and everybody in the place had a great respect for him, for he was a fine priest in the parish. He was like this for a good while, until a day came when he went to visit a great gentleman who was in that place; just as yourself might come into this garden,[1] or like that, and they were walking outside

---
[1] This story was told to me in the garden of Mr. Reddington Roche, at Rye Hill.

in the garden, the gentleman and himself. When he was going up a walk in this garden a lady met him, and when she was passing the priest on the walk, she struck a light little blow of her hand on his cheek. It was that lady who had been hanged who was in it, but the priest did not recognise her, [seemingly] alive, and thought she was some other fine lady who was there.

She went then into a summer house, and the priest went in after her, and had a little conversation with her, and it is likely that she beguiled him with melodious conversation and talk before she went out. When she herself and he himself were ready to depart, and when they were separating from one another, she turned to him and said, " you ought to recognize me," said she, " I am the woman that you hanged ; I told you that day that I would have you yet, and I shall. I came to you now to damn you." With that she vanished out of his sight.

He gave himself up then ; he said that he was damned for ever. He was getting no rest, either by day or by night, with the fear that was on him at her having met him again. He said that it was not in his power either to go back or forward—that he was to be damned for ever. That thought was preying on him day and night.

He went away then, and he went to the Bishop, and he told him the whole story and made his confession to him, and told him how she met him and tempted him. Then the bishop told him that he was damned for ever, and that there was nothing in the world to save him or able to save him.

" I have no hope at all, so ? " said the priest.

The bishop said to him, " you have no hope at all, till you get a small load of cambrick needles,"—the finest needles at all—" and get a ship, and go out to sea, and according as you go every hundred yards on the sea you must throw away a needle from you out of the ship. Be going then," says he, " for ever," says he, "until you have thrown away the last of them. Unless you are able to gather them up out of the sea and to bring them all to me back again here, you will be lost for ever."

"Well that's a thing that I never shall do; it fails me to do that," said the priest.

He got the ship and the needles and went out to sea. according as he used to go a piece he used to throw a needle from him. He was going until he was very far away from land, and until he had thrown out the last needle. By the time he had thrown away the last needle, his own food was used up, and he had not a thing to eat. He spent three days then, on end, without bite or sup or drink, or means to come by them.

Then on the third day he saw dry land over from him at a distance. "I shall go," said he, "to yon dry land over there, and perhaps we may get something there that we can eat." The man was on the road to be lost. He drew towards the place and walked out upon the dry land. He spent from twelve o'clock in the day walking until it was eight o'clock at night. Then when the night had fallen black, he found himself in a great wood, and he saw a light at a distance from him in the wood, and he drew towards it. There were twelve little girls there before him and they had a good fire, and he asked of them a morsel to eat for God's sake. Something to eat was got ready for him. After that he got a good supper, and when he had the supper eaten he began to talk to them, telling them how he had left home and what it was he had done out of the way, and the penance that had been put on him by the bishop, and how he had to go out to sea and throw the needles from him.

"God help you, poor man," said one of the women, "it was a hard penance that was put upon you."

Says he, "I am afraid that I shall never go home. I have no hope of it. Have you any idea at all for me down from heaven as to where I shall get a man who will tell me whether I shall save myself from the sins that I have committed?"

"I don't know," said a little girl of them, "but we have mass in this house every day in the year at twelve o'clock. A priest comes here to read mass for us, and unless that priest is able to tell it to you there is no use in your going back for ever."

The poor man was tired then and he went to sleep. Well now, he was that tired that he never felt to get up, and never heard the priest in the house reading mass until the mass was read and priest gone. He awoke then and asked one of the women had the priest come yet. She told him that he had and that he had read mass and was gone again. He was greatly troubled and sorry then after the priest.

Now with fear lest he might not awake next day, he brought in a harrow and he lay down on the harrow in such a way that he would have no means, as he thought, of getting any repose.

But in spite of all that the sleep preyed on him so much that he never felt to get up until mass was read and the priest gone the second day. Now he had two days lost, and the girls told him that unless he got the priest the third day he would have to go away from themselves. He went out then and brought in a bed of briars on which were thorns to wound his skin, and he lay down on them without his shirt in the corner, and with all sorts of torture that he was putting on himself he kept himself awake throughout the night until the priest came. The priest read mass, and when he had it read and he going away, my poor man went up to him and asked him to remain, that he had a story to tell him, and he told him then the way in which he was, and the penance that was on him, and how he had left home, and how he had thrown the needles behind him into the sea, and all that he had gone through of every kind.

It was a saint who was in the priest who read mass, and when he heard all that the other priest had to tell him, " to-morrow," says the saint to him, " go up to such and such a street that was in the town in that country; there is a woman there," says he, " selling fish, and the first fish you take hold of bring it with you. Fourpence the woman will want from you for the fish, and here is the fourpence to give her. And when you have the fish bought, open it up, and there is never a needle of all you threw into the sea that is not inside in its stomach. Leave the fish there behind you, everything you want is in its stomach; bring the needles with you, but leave the fish." The saint went away from him then.

The priest went to that street where the woman was selling fish, as the saint had ordered, and he brought the first fish he took hold of, and opened it up and took out the thing which was in its stomach, and he found the needles there as the saint had said to him. He brought them with him and he left the fish behind him. He turned back until he came to the house again. He spent the night there until morning. He rose next day, and when he had his meal eaten he left his blessing to the women and faced for his own home.

He was travelling then until he came to his own home. When the bishop who had put the penance on him heard that he had come back he went to visit him.

" You have come home?" said the bishop.

" I have," said he.

" And the needles with you?" said the bishop.

" Yes," says the priest, " here they are."

" Why then, the sins that are on me," said the bishop, " are greater than those on you."

The bishop had no rest then until he went to the Pope, and he told him that he had put this penance on the priest, " and I had no expectation that he would come back for ever until he was drowned," said he.

" That same penance that you put upon the priest you must put it on yourself now," said the Pope, " and you must make the same journey. The man is holy," said he.

The bishop went away, and embarked upon the same journey, and never came back since.

# THE FRIARS OF URLAUR

IN times long ago there was a House of Friars on the brink of Loch Urlaur but there is nothing in it now except the old walls, with the water of the lake beating up against them every day in the year that the wind be's blowing from the south.

Whilst the friars were living in that house there was happiness in Ireland, and many is the youth who got good instructions from the friars in that house, who is now a saint in heaven.

It was the custom of the people of the villages to gather one day in the year to a "pattern," in the place where there used to be fighting and great slaughter when the Firbolgs were in Ireland, but the friars used to be amongst the young people to give them a good example and to keep them from fighting and quarrelling. There used to be pipers, fiddlers, harpers and bards at the pattern, along with trump-players and music-horns; young and old used to be gathered there, and there used to be songs, music, dancing and sport amongst them.

But there was a change to come and it came heavy. Some evil spirit found out its way to Loch Urlaur. It came at first in the shape of a black boar, with tusks on it as long as a pike, and as sharp as the point of a needle

One day the friars went out to walk on the brink of the lake. There was a chair cut out of the rock about twenty feet from the brink, and what should they see seated in the chair but the big black boar. They did not know what was in it. Some of them said that it was a great water-dog that was in it, but they were not long in doubt about it, for it let a screech out of it that was heard seven miles on each side of it; it rose up then on its hind feet and was there screeching and dancing for a couple of hours. Then it leaped into the water, and no sooner did it do that than there rose an awful storm which swept the roof off the friar's house, and off every other house within seven miles of the place. Furious waves rose upon the lake which sent the water twenty feet up into the air. Then came the lightning and the thunder, and everybody thought that it was the end of the world that was in it. There was such a great darkness that a person could not see his own hand if he were to put it out before him.

The friars went in and fell to saying prayers, but it was not long till they had company. The great black boar came in, opened its mouth, and cast out of it a litter of bonhams. These began on the instant running backwards and forwards and screeching as loud as if there were the seven deaths on them with the hunger. There was fear and astonishment on the friars, and they did not know what they ought to do. The abbot came forward and desired them to bring him holy water. They did so, and as soon as he sprinkled a drop of it on the boar and on the bonhams they went out in a blaze of fire, sweeping part of the side-wall with them into the lake. "A thousand thanks to God," said the Father Abbot, "the devil is gone from us."

But my grief! he did not go far. When the darkness departed they went to the brink of the lake, and they saw the black boar sitting in the stone chair that was cut out in the rock.

"Get me my curragh," said the Father Abbot, "and I'll banish the thief."

They got him the curragh and holy water, and two of them went into the curragh with him, but as soon as they came near to the black boar he leaped into the water, the storm rose, and the furious waves, and the curragh and the three who were in it were thrown high up upon the land with broken bones.

They sent for a doctor and for the bishop, and when they told the story to the bishop he said, "There is a limb of the devil in the shape of a friar amongst you, but I'll find him out without delay." Then he ordered them all to come forward, and when they came he called out the name of every friar, and according as each answered he was put on one side. But when he called out the name of Friar Lucas he was not to be found. He sent a messenger for him, but could get no account of him. At last the friar they were seeking for came to the door, flung down a cross that he had round his neck, smote his foot on it, and burst into a great laugh, turned on his heel, and into the lake. When he came as far as the chair on the rock he sat on it, whipped off his friar's clothes and flung them out into the water. When he stripped himself they saw that there was hair on him from the sole of his foot to the top of his head, as long as a goat's beard. He was not long alone, the black boar came to him from the bottom of the lake, and they began romping and dancing on the rock.

Then the bishop enquired what place did the rogue come from, and the (father) Superior said that he came a month ago from the north, and that he had a friar's dress on him when he came, and that he asked no account from him of what brought him to this place.

"You are too blind to be a Superior," said the bishop, "since you do not recognise a devil from a friar." While the bishop was talking the eyes of everyone present were on him, and they did not feel till the black boar came behind them and the rogue that had been a friar riding on him. "Seize the villain, seize him," says the bishop.

"You didn't seize me yourself," says the villain, "when

I was your pet hound, and when you were giving me the meat that you would not give to the poor people who were weak with the hunger; I thank you for it, and I'll have a hot corner for you when you leave this world."

Some of them were afraid, but more of them made an attempt to catch the black boar and its rider, but they went into the lake, sat on the rock, and began screaming so loud that they made the bishop and the friars deaf, so that they could not hear one word from one another, and they remained so during their life, and that is the reason they were called the " Deaf Friars," and from that day (to this) the old saying is in the mouth of the people, " You're as deaf as a friar of Urlaur."

The black boar gave no rest to the friars either by night or day : he himself, and the rogue of a companion that he had, were persecuting them in many a way, and neither they themselves nor the bishop were able to destroy or banish them.

At last they were determining on giving up the place altogether, but the bishop said to them to have patience till he would take counsel with Saint Gerald, the patron saint of Mayo. The bishop went to the saint and told him the story from beginning to end. " That sorrowful occurrence did not take place in my county," said the saint, " and I do not wish to have any hand in it." At this time Saint Gerald was only a higher priest in Tirerrill (?) but anything he took in hand succeeded with him, for he was a saint on earth from his youth. He told the bishop that he would be in Urlaur, at the end of a week, and that he would make an attempt to banish the evil spirit.

The bishop returned and told the friars what Gerald had said, and that message gave them great courage. They spent that week saying prayers, but the end of the week came, and another week went by, and Saint Gerald did not come, for " not as is thought does it happen." Gerald was struck with illness as it was fated for him, and he could not come.

One night the friars had a dream, and it was not one man alone who had it, but every man in the house. In the dream each man saw a woman clothed in white linen, and she said to them that it was not in the power of any man living to banish the evil spirit except of a piper named Donagh O'Grady who is living at Tavraun, a man who did more good, says she, on this world than all the priests and friars in the country.

On the morning of the next day, after the matin prayers, the Superior said, " I was dreaming, friars, last night about the evil spirit of the lake, and there was a ghost or an angel present who said to me that it was not in the power of any man living to banish the evil spirit except of a piper whose name was Donagh O'Grady who is living at Tavraun, a man who did more good in this world than all the priests and friars in the country."

" I had the same dream too," says every man of them.

" It is against our faith to believe in dreams," says the Superior, " but this was more than a dream, I saw an angel beside my bed clothed in white linen."

" Indeed I saw the same thing," says every man of them.

" It was a messenger from God who was in it," said the Superior, and with that he desired two friars to go for the piper. They went to Tavraun to look for him and they found him in a drinking-house half drunk. They asked him to come with them to the Superior of the friars at Urlaur.

" I'll not go one foot out of this place till I get my pay," says the piper. " I was at a wedding last night and I was not paid yet."

" Take our word that you will be paid," said the friars.

"I won't take any man's word; money down, or I'll stop where I am." There was no use in talk or flattery, they had to return home again without the piper.

They told their story to the Superior, and he gave them money to go back for the piper. They went to Tavraun again, gave the money to the piper and asked him to come with them.

"Wait till I drink another naggin; I can't play hearty music till I have my enough drunk?"

"We won't ask you to play music, it's another business we have for you."

O'Grady drank a couple of naggins, put the pipes under his oxter (arm-pit) and said, "I'm ready to go with ye now."

"Leave the pipes behind you," said the friars, "you won't want them."

"I wouldn't leave my pipes behind me if it was to Heaven I was going," says the piper.

When the piper came into the presence of the Superior, the Superior began examining him about the good works he had done during his life.

"I never did any good work during my life that I have any remembrance of," said the piper.

"Did you give away any alms during your life?" said the Superior.

"Indeed, I remember now, that I did give a tenpenny piece to a daughter of Mary O'Donnell's one night. She was in great want of the tenpenny piece, and she was going to sell herself to get it, when I gave it to her. After a little while she thought about the mortal sin she was going to commit, she gave up the world and its temptations and went into a convent, and people say that she passed a pious life. She died about seven years ago, and I heard that there were angels playing melodious music in the room when she was dying, and it's a pity I wasn't listening to them, for I'd have the tune now!"

"Well," said the Superior, "there's an evil spirit in the lake outside that's persecuting us day and night, and we had a revelation from an angel who came to us in a dream, that there was not a man alive able to banish the evil spirit but you."

"A male angel or female?" says the piper.

"It was a woman we saw," says the Superior, "she was dressed in white linen."

"Then I'll bet you five tenpenny pieces that it was Mary O'Donnell's daughter was in it," says the piper.

"It is not lawful for us to bet," says the Superior, "but if you banish the evil spirit of the lake you will get twenty tenpenny pieces."

"Give me a couple of naggins of good whiskey to give me courage," says the piper.

"There is not a drop of spirits in the house," says the Superior, "you know that we don't taste it at all."

"Unless you give me a drop to drink," says the piper, "go and do the work yourself."

They had to send for a couple of naggins, and when the piper drank it he said that he was ready, and asked them to show him the evil spirit. They went to the brink of the lake, and they told him that the evil spirit used to come on to the rock every time that they struck the bell to announce the "Angel's Welcome" [Angelical Salutation].

"Go and strike it now," says the piper.

The friars went, and began to strike the bell, and it was not long till the black boar and its rider came swimming to the rock. When they got up on the rock the boar let a loud screech, and the rogue began dancing.

The piper looked at them and said, "wait till I give ye music." With that he squeezed on his pipes, and began playing, and on the moment the black boar and its rider leapt into the lake and made for the piper. He was thinking of running away, when a great white dove came out of the sky over the boar and its rider, shot lightning down on top of them and killed them. The waves threw them up on the brink of the lake, and the piper went and told the Superior and the friars that the evil spirit of the lake and its rider were dead on the shore.

They all came out, and when they saw that their enemies were dead they uttered three shouts for excess of joy. They did not know then what they would do with the corpses. They gave forty tenpenny pieces to the piper and told him to throw the bodies into a hole far from the house. The piper got a lot of tinkers who were going the way and gave them ten tenpenny pieces to throw the corpse into a deep hole in a shaking-scraw a mile from the house of the friars. They took up the corpses, the piper walked out before them playing music, and they never stopped till they cast the bodies into the hole, and the shaking-scraw closed over them and nobody ever saw them since. The " Hole of the Black Boar " is to be seen still. The piper and the tinkers went to the public house, and they were drinking till they were drunk, then they began fighting, and you may be certain that the piper did not come out of Urlaur with a whole skin.

The friars built up the walls and the roof of the house and passed prosperous years in it, until the accursed foreigners came who banished the friars and threw down the greater part of the house to the ground.

The piper died a happy death, and it was the opinion of the people that he went to Heaven, and that it may be so with us all!

# SHAUN THE TINKER

They were poor, both of them, the man and his wife. The man had no other means in the world except his day's pay, going here and going there, and earning his day's wages from place to place.

The beginning of the harvest was come now, and he went in to the wife and said to her—Elleesh was the wife's name—"Elleesh," says he, "stand up," says he, "and make ready my meal for me until I go to Kildare to-morrow."

Elleesh got ready the meal for him as well as ever she was able, and she washed him and tidied him up and put good clean trousers on him, and himself got ready to be going. And the poor man did go, off he went. He had no provisions going away then, only four shillings to pay his way.

He was going then and journeying until he came to the top of a bridge, and there he met with a stumble and was thrown on one knee. "Oh, musha," says he, "the devil break my neck when I'll pass this way again."

He went on then and he never stopped until he came into Kildare, and he settled with a farmer there and spent four years with him without coming home at all. He never took one penny from the farmer in the course of the four years except as much as put clothing on him. Now at the end of the four years he took it into his head to be going home again.

And this was what he was getting in the year—five pounds. And likely enough, when he took it into his head to be going, that he said to the farmer and to the farmer's wife that he was to be departing in the morning. They gave him his share of money then. Then he made for home, and fifteen pounds was what he had coming home of him. He never spent but five pounds on his clothes all the time he was with the farmer.

He was coming and ever-coming along the road until he came to a corner where four roads met. A poor man met him and asked alms of him. "God salute you," says he.

"God and Mary salute you," says Shaun.

"In Kildare you were," says he.

"Well, yes," says Shaun.

"You have money so," says he, "and I am asking my alms of you in honour of God and of Mary."

"He gave him alms then—five pounds he gave him. "Now Shaun," says the poor man, when he was going away from him. "I don't like you to go away without giving you [your] earned reward for your five pounds. "What is the thing that you most wish for?"

"Anything that I desire," says Shaun, "me to have lots of money for it in my pocket. And anything that would be putting trouble on me, me to have leave to shut it up in this bottle which I have in my hand."

"You'll get that," says he.

He was going along then until he came to the corner of four other roads and another poor man met him. "God salute you," says the poor man. "God and Mary salute you." "You were in Kildare," said the poor man. "That's the place I was," says Shaun. "If you are coming back out of Kildare you're not without money, and I am asking my alms of you in honour of God and Mary. "It's short till I have my money spent," says Shaun. "But here," says he, putting the hand in his pocket, "here's five pounds for you."

When he gave it to him, the poor man said, "I don't

like you to go away without giving you a reward for your five pounds. What sort of a thing is it that you'd like best to have?" "Any person that would be doing anything at all out of the way with me [me to be able] to put him into my budget and him to remain there until myself would give him leave to go away, or until myself would let him out. "You'll have that to get," says he.

He went away, then, and he was travelling until he went where four other roads met. There was another poor man before him there. "This is the third man," says Shaun. "God salute you, Tinker Shaun," says he as soon as Shaun came up with him. "God and Mary salute you." "You're coming out of Kildare, Shaun," says he. "I am, indeed," says Shaun. But he said to himself, "Isn't it well how every man recognises me and without me recognising them." "I am asking my alms of you in honour of God and of Mary if you have any money with you coming from Kildare." "Oh, musha, I'll give you that and my blessing. I met another pair before this and I gave five pounds to each man of them, and here's five pounds for you." "I don't like you to go away Shaun without your reward, and what is the thing you'd have most desire for?" "Well, then," says Shaun, "when I was at home I had an apple tree in the garden at the back of the house, and I used to be troubled with gossoons coming there and stealing the apples. I should like, since I am going home again now, that every person except myself who shall lay his hand on that tree that his hand should stick to it, and that he should have no power of himself to go away without leave from me. "You'll get that Shaun," says he.

He was travelling then until he came to the bridge where he had stumbled as he was going to Kildare the time he was thrown on one knee. Who should be standing on the bridge before him but the Devil. "Who are you?" says Tinker Shaun. "I am the Devil," says he.

"And what sent you here?" says Shaun.

"Well," says he, "when you went this way before didn't you say that if you were to go this way again might the Devil break your neck?"

"I said that," says Shaun.

"Well, I've come before you now that I may break your neck."

"Try if you can," said Shaun. The Devil moved over towards him and was going to kill him, when Shaun said, "In with you into my bag this moment and don't be troubling me." The Devil had to go into the bag because Shaun had that power.

Shaun was going along then, and the Devil in the bag slung over his back. When he came to the next bridge he stood to take a rest and there were two women washing there. "I'll give ye five pounds and give my bag a good dressing with the beetles." They began beating it. "The bag is harder than the Devil himself," say they. "It is the Devil himself that's in it," says Shaun, "and lay on him." They beat it really then until they gave him enough.

He threw it up over his back then and off he went until he came to a forge. He went into the forge. "I'll give you five pounds," says he to the smith, "and strike a good spell on this bag." There were two smiths there and they began leathering the bag. "Why, then," says one of the smiths, "your bag is harder than the Devil himself:" "It is the Devil himself that's in it," says Shaun, "and lay on him, ye, and beat him." One of the men put a hole in the bag with the blow he gave it and he looked in on the hole and he saw the Devil's eye at the hole. The poker was in the fire and it red hot The smith stuck it into the hole in such a way that he put it into the Devil's eye, and that's the thing which has left the old Devil half blind ever since.

He raised the bag on his back then, and he was going away when the Devil rose up and burst the bag and departed from him. Shaun came home.

At the end of a quarter of a year when Shaun was at home with the wife the Devil came to him again " You must come with me, Shaun," says he ; " make your soul," says he, " I'll give you death without respite."

" I'll go with you," says Shaun ; " but give me respite until to-morrow until I have everything ready, and I'll go with you then and welcome."

' I won't give you any respite at all ; neither a day nor an hour, you thief."

" I won't ask you for any respite," says Shaun, " only as long as I would be eating a single apple off that tree. Pull me one yourself, and I'll be with you."

The old Devil moved over to the tree, and took hold of a branch to pluck an apple off it and he stuck to the branch, and was not able to loose himself. He remained there on the branch during seven years.

One day that Shaun was in the garden again by himself he was not thinking, but he went gathering a bundle of kippeens for Elleesh, to make a fire for her, and what was the branch it should fall to him to cut for Elleesh but the branch in which the Devil was. The Devil gave a leap into the air. " Now Shaun," says he, " be ready ; you will never go either forward nor back. You must come with me on the spot."

" Well I'll go," says Shaun ; "I'll go with you," says he ; " but it's a long time we are at odds with one another, and we ought to have a drink together. Elleesh has a good bottle and come in till we drink a drop of it before we go." "Why, then, I'll go with you," says the Devil, as there was the Devil's thirst on him after his being up in the tree so long. They drank their enough then inside in Elleesh's hovel, and when the Devil had the bottle empty he rose up standing, that he might get a grip of Shaun's throat to choke him. "In with you into the bottle," says Shaun. "In with you this moment," says he. "Did you think that you would play on me," says he. The Devil had to go into the bottle, and he spent seven years inside the bottle, with Shaun, without being let out.

Now it fell out that Elleesh had a young son, and there was a bottle wanting to go for stuff for Elleesh. What was the bottle they should bring with them but the bottle in which the Devil was down, and when they took the cork out of it the Devil went off with himself.

Shaun was gone away looking for gossips for his son. The Son of God met him.

"God salute you, Shaun," says he.

"God and Mary salute you."

"Where were you going now, Shaun?" says he.

"I was hunting for gossips for my son," says Shaun.

"Would you give him to me, and I'll stand for him?"

"Who are you?" says Tinker Shaun.

"I am the Son of God" says he.

"Well, then, indeed, I won't give him to you," says Shaun, "you give seven times their enough to some people, and you don't give their half enough to other people."

The Son of God departed.

The King of Sunday met him then and they saluted one another.

"Where were you going?" says the King of Sunday.

"Well, then, I was going hunting for a gossip for my son."

"Will you give him to me?" says the King of Sunday.

"Who are you?" says Shaun.

"I am the King of Sunday."

"Indeed, then, I won't give him," says Shaun. "You have only a single day in the week and you're not able to do much good that day itself."

In this way he refused him, and the King of Sunday departed from him.

Who should meet him then and he coming home but the Death. [The Devil was afraid to go near him again, but he sent the Death to meet him.] "Make your soul now Shaun," says he, "I have you."

"Oh, you wouldn't give me death now," says Shaun, "until I baptise my son."

"All right, baptise him," said the Death. "Who will you put to stand for him?"

"I don't see any person," says Shaun, "better than yourself. It's you who will leave him longest alive," says he.

When he got the son baptised he gave death to Shaun. He would not allow him to be humbugging him.

# THE STUDENT WHO LEFT COLLEGE

THERE came a number of young people from the County of Galway, to a great college, to learn and gain instruction, so as to become priests. I often heard the name of this college from my mother, but I do not remember it. It was not Maynooth. There was a man of these of the name of Patrick O'Flynn. He was the son of a rich farmer. His father and his mother desired to make a priest of him. He was a nice, gentle lad. He used not to go dancing with the other boys in the evening, but it was his habit to go out with the grey-light of day, and he used to be walking by himself up and down under the shadow of the great trees that were round about the college, and he used to remain there thinking and meditating by himself, until some person would come to bring him into his room.

One evening, in the month of May, he went out, as was his custom, and he was taking his walk under the trees when he heard a melodious music. There came a darkness or a sort of blindness over his eyes, and when he found his sight again he beheld a great high wall on every side of him, and out in front of him a shining road. The musicians were on the road, and they playing melodiously, and he heard a voice saying, "*Come with us to the land of delight and rest.*" He looked back and beheld a great high wall behind him and on each side of him, and he was not able to return back again across the wall, although he desired to return. He went forward then after the music. He did not know how long he walked, but the great high wall kept ever on each side of him and behind him.

He was going and ever-going, until they came to a great

river, and water in it as red as blood. Wonder came upon him then, and great fear. But the musicians walked across the river without wetting their feet, and Patrick O'Flynn followed them without wetting his own. He thought at first that the musicians belonged to the Fairy-Host, and next he thought that he had died and that it was a group of angels that were in it, taking him to heaven.

The walls fell away from them then, on each side, and they came to a great wide plain. They were going then, and ever-going, until they came to a fine castle that was in the midst of the plain. The musicians went in, but Patrick O'Flynn remained outside. It was not long until the chief of the musicians came out to him and brought him into a handsome chamber. He spoke not a word, and Patrick O'Flynn never heard one word spoken so long as he remained there.

There was no night in that place, but the light of day throughout. He never ate and he never drank a single thing there, and he never saw anyone eating or drinking, and the music never ceased. Every half-hour, as he thought, he used to hear a bell, as it were a church-bell, being rung, but he never beheld the bell, and he was unable to see it in any place.

When the musicians used to go out upon the plain before the castle, there used to come a tribe of every sort of bird in the heavens, playing the most melodious music that ear ever heard. It was often Patrick O'Flynn said to himself, " It is certain that I am in heaven, but is it not curious that I have no remembrance of sickness, nor of death, nor of judgment, and that I have not seen God nor His Blessed Mother, as is promised to us ? "

Patrick O'Flynn did not know how long he was in that delightful place. He thought that he had been in it only for a short little time, but he was in it for a hundred years and one.

One day the musicians were out in the field and he was listening to them, when the chief came to him. He brought him out and put him behind the musicians. They departed on their way, and they made neither stop nor stay until they came to the river that was as red as blood. They went across that, without wetting their foot-soles, and went forward until they came to the field near the college where they found him at the first. Then they departed out of his sight like a mist.

He looked round him, and recognised the college, but he thought that the trees were higher and that there was some change in the college itself. He went in, then, but he did not recognise a single person whom he met, and not a person recognised him.

The principal of the college came to him, and said to him, " Where are you from, son, or what is your name ? "

" I am Patrick O'Flynn from the County of Galway," said he.

" How long are you here ? " said the principal.

" I am here since the first day of March," said he.

" I think that you are out of your senses," said the principal, " there is no person of your name in the college, and there has not been for twenty years, for I am more than twenty years here."

" Though you were in it since you were born, yet I am here since last March, and I can show you my room and my books."

With that he went up the stairs, and the principal after him. He went into his room and looked round him, and said, " This is my room, but that is not my furniture, and those are not my books that are in it." He saw an old bible upon the table and he opened it, and said : " This is my bible, my mother gave it to me when I was coming here ; and, see, my name is written in it."

The principal looked at the bible, and there, as sure as God is in heaven, was the name of Patrick O'Flynn written in it, and the day of the month that he left home.

Now there was great trouble of mind on the principal, and he did not know what he should do. He sent for the masters and the professors and told them the story.

" By my word," said an old priest that was in it, " I heard talk when I was young, of a student who went away out of this college, and there was no account of him since, whether living or dead. The people searched the river and the bog holes, but there was no account to be had of him, and they never got the body."

The principal called to them then and bade them bring him a great book in which the name of every person was written who had come to that college since it was founded. He looked through the book, and see ! Patrick O'Flynn's name was in it, and the day of the month that he came, and this [note] was written opposite to his name, that the same Patrick O'Flynn had departed on such a day, and that nobody knew what had become of him. Now it was exactly one hundred and one years from the day he went until the day he came back in that fashion.

" This is a wonderful, and a very wonderful story," said the principal, " but, do you wait here quietly my son," said he, " and I shall write to the bishop." He did that, and he got an account from the bishop to keep the man until he should come himself.

At the end of a week after that the bishop came and sent for Patrick O'Flynn. There was nobody present except the two. " Now, son," said the bishop, " go on your knees and make a confession." Then he made an act of contrition, and the bishop gave him absolution.

Immediately there came a fainting and a heavy sleep over him, and he was, as it were, for three days and three nights a dead person. When he came to himself the bishop and priests were round about him. He rose up, shook himself, and told them his story, as I have it told, and he put excessive wonder upon every man of them. "Now," said he, "here I am alive and safe, and do as ye please."

The bishop and the priests took counsel together. "It is a saintly man you are," said the bishop then, "and we shall give you holy orders on the spot."

They made a priest of him then, and no sooner were holy orders given him than he fell dead upon the altar, and they all heard at the same time the most melodious music that ear ever listened to, above them in the sky, and they all said that it was the angels who were in it, carrying the soul of Father O'Flynn up to heaven with them.

# THE OLD WOMAN OF BEARE

There was an old woman in it, and long ago it was, and if we had been there that time we would not be here now ; we would have a new story or an old story, and that would not be more likely than to be without any story at all.

The hag was very old, and she herself did not know her own age, nor did anybody else. There was a friar and his boy journeying one day, and they came in to the house of the Old Woman of Beare.

" God save you," said the friar.

" The same man save yourself," said the hag ; " you're welcome,[1] sit down at the fire and warm yourself."

The friar sat down, and when he had well finished warming himself he began to talk and discourse with the old hag.

" If it's no harm of me to ask it of you, I'd like to know your age, because I know you are very old " [said the friar].

" It is no harm at all to ask me," said the hag ; " I'll answer you as well as I can. There is never a year since I came to age that I used not to kill a beef, and throw the bones of the beef up on the loft which is above your head. If you wish to know my age you can send your boy up on the loft and count the bones.

True was the tale. The friar sent the boy up on the loft and the boy began counting the bones, and with all the bones that were on the loft he had no room on the loft itself to count them, and he told the friar that he would

---

[1] Literally. ' He (*i.e.*, God) is your life " ; the equivalent of " hail ! " " welcome."

have to throw the bones down on the floor—that there was no room on the loft.

"Down with them," said the friar, "and I'll keep count of them from below."

The boy began throwing them down from above and the friar began writing down [the number], until he was about tired out, and he asked the boy had he them nearly counted, and the boy answered the friar down from the loft that he had not even one corner of the loft emptied yet.

"If that's the way of it, come down out of the loft and throw the bones up again," said the friar

The boy came down, and he threw up the bones, and [so] the friar was [just] as wise coming in as he was going out.

"Though I don't know your age," said the friar to the hag, "I know that you haven't lived up to this time without seeing marvellous things in the course of your life, and the greatest marvel that you ever saw—tell it to me, if you please."

"I saw one marvel which made me wonder greatly," said the hag.

"Recount it to me," said the Friar, "if you please."

"I myself and my girl were out one day, milking the cows, and it was a fine, lovely day, and I was just after milking one of the cows, and when I raised my head I looked round towards my left hand, and I saw a great blackness coming over my head in the air. "Make haste," says myself to the girl, "until we milk the cows smartly, or we'll be wet and drowned before we reach home, with the rain." I was on the pinch[1] of my life and so was my girl, to have the cows milked before we'd get the

---

[1] Literally, "the boiling of the angles-between-the-fingers was on me."

shower, for I thought myself that it was a shower that was coming, but on my raising my head again I looked round me and beheld a woman coming as white as the swan that is on the brink of the waves. She went past me like a blast of wind, and the wind that was before her she was overtaking it, and the wind that was behind her, it could not come up with her. It was not long till I saw after the woman two mastiffs, and two yards of their tongue twisted round their necks, and balls of fire out of their mouths, and I wondered greatly at that. And after the dogs I beheld a black coach and a team of horses drawing it, and there were balls of fire on every side out of the coach, and as the coach was going past me the beasts stood and something that was in the coach uttered from it an unmeaning sound, and I was terrified, and faintness came over me, and when I came back out of the faint I heard the voice in the coach again, asking me had I seen anything going past me since I came there; and I told him as I am telling you, and I asked him who he was himself, or what was the meaning of the woman and the mastiffs which went by me.

"I am the Devil, and those are two mastiffs which I sent after that soul."

"And is it any harm for me to ask," says I, "what is the crime the woman did when she was in the world?"

"That is a woman," said the Devil, "who brought scandal upon a priest, and she died in a state of deadly sin, and she did not repent of it, and unless the mastiffs come up with her before she comes to the gates of Heaven the glorious Virgin will come and will ask a request of her only Son to grant the woman forgiveness for her sins, and the Virgin will obtain pardon for her, and I'll be out of her. But if the mastiffs come up with her before she goes to Heaven she is mine."

The great Devil drove on his beasts, and went out of my sight, and myself and my girl came home, and I was heavy, and tired and sad at remembering the vision which I saw, and I was greatly astonished at that wonder, and I lay in my bed for three days, and the fourth day I arose very done up and feeble, and not without cause, since any woman who would see the wonder that I saw, she would be grey a hundred years before her term of life[1] was expired.

"Did you ever see any other marvel in your time?" says the friar to the hag.

"A week after leaving my bed I got a letter telling me that one of my friends was dead, and that I would have to go to the funeral. I proceeded to the funeral, and on my going into the corpse-house the body was in the coffin, and the coffin was laid down on the bier, and four men went under the bier that they might carry the coffin, and they weren't able to even stir[2] the bier off the ground. And another four men came, and they were not able to move it off the ground. They were coming, man after man, until twelve came, and went under the bier, and they weren't able to lift it.

"I spoke myself, and I asked the people who were at the funeral what sort of trade had this man when he was in the world, and it was told me that it was a herd he was. And I asked of the people who were there was there any other herd at the funeral. Then there came four men that nobody at all who was at the funeral had any knowledge or recognition of, and they told me that they were four herds, and they went under the bier and they lifted it as you would lift a handful of chaff, and off they went as quick and sharp as ever they could lift a foot. Good powers of walking they had, and a fine long step I had

---

[1] Literally, "before her age being spent." [2] Literally, "give it wind."

myself, and I cut out after them, and not a mother's son knew what the place was to which they were departing with the body, and we were going and ever going until the night and the day were parting from one another, until the night was coming black dark dreadful, until the grey horse was going under the shadow of the docking and until the docking was going fleeing before him.[1]

> The roots going under the ground,
> The leaves going into the air,
> The grey horse a-fleeing apace,
> And I left lonely there.

"On looking round me, there wasn't one of all the funeral behind me, except two others. The other people were done up, and they were not able to come half way, some of them fainted and some of them died. Going forward two steps more in front of me I was within in a dark wood wet and cold, and the ground opened, and I was swallowed down into a black dark hole without a mother's son or a father's daughter[2] next nor near me, without a man to be had to keen me or to lay me out; so that I threw myself on my two knees, and I was there throughout four days sending my prayer up to God to take me out of that speedily and quickly. And with the fourth day there came a little hole like the eye of a needle on one corner of the abode where I was; and I was a-praying always and the hole was a-growing in size day by day, and on the seventh day it increased to such a size that I got out through it. I took to my heels[3] then when I got my feet with me on the outside [of the hole] going home. The distance which I walked in one single day

---

[1] The fairies ride their little grey horses, and stable them at night under the leaves of the copóg or dock-leaf, or docking. But if they arrive too late and night has fallen, then the copóg has folded her leaves and will not shelter them.

[2] Literally, "man's daughter."

[3] Literally, "I gave to the soles." Many people still say in speaking English, "I gave to the butts." The Irish word means butt as well as sole.

following the coffin, I spent five weeks coming back the same road, and don't you see yourself now that I got cause to be withered, old, aged, grey, and my life to be shortening through those two perils in which I was."

"You're a fine, hardy old woman all the time," said the friar.

# FRIAR BRIAN

There was a young man in it long ago, and long ago it was, and he had a great love for card-playing and drinking whiskey. He came short [at last] of money, and he did not know what he would do without money.

A man met him, and he going home in the night. "I often see you going home this road," said the man to him.

"There's no help for it now," says he; "I have no money."

"Now," says the man, "I'll give you money every time you'll want it, if you will give to me written with your own blood [a writing to say] that you are mine such and such a year, at the end of one and twenty years."

It was the Devil who was in it in the shape of a man.

He gave it to him written with his share of blood that he would be his at the end of one and twenty years.

He had money then every time ever he wanted it until the one and twenty years were almost out, and then fear began coming on him. He went to the priest and he told it [all] to him. "I could not do any good for you," says the priest. "You must go to such and such a man who is going into Ellasthrum (?) He has so much of the Devil's influence (?) that he does be able to change round the castle door any time the wind is blowing [too hard] on it."

He went to this man and he told him his story. "I wouldn't be able to do you any good," says he, "you must go to Friar Brian."

He went to Friar Brian and told him his story. The one and twenty years were all but up by this time. " Here is a stick for you," said Friar Brian, " and cut a ring [with the stick] round about the place where you'll stand. He [the Devil] won't be able to come inside the place which you'll cut out with this stick. And do you be arguing with him, and I'll be watching you both," says he. " Tell him that there must be some judgment [passed] on the case before you depart [to go away] with him."

" Very well," says the man.

When the appointed hour came the man was standing in the place he said. The Devil came to him. He told the man that the time was up and that he had to come along.

The man began to say that the time was not up. He cut a ring round about himself with the stick which Friar Brian had given him. " Well, then," says the man, says he [at last], " we'll leave it to the judgment of the first person who shall come past us."

" I am satisfied," says the Diabhac.[1]

Friar Brian came to the place where they were. " What is it all about from the beginning ? " says Friar Brian. The Diabhac told him that he had this man bought for one and twenty years, and that he had to come with him to-day ; " it is left to you to judge the case."

" Now," says Friar Brian, says he, " if you were to go to a fair to buy a cow or a horse, and if you gave earnest money for it, wouldn't you say that it was more just for you to have it than for the man who would come in the evening and who would buy it without paying any earnest money for it ? "

" I say," says the Diabhac, " that the man who paid

---

[1] Diabhac, pronounced in Connaught, d'youc; a homonym for the more direct diabhal—devil, as " deil " in English.

earnest money for it first, ought to get it."

" And now," says Friar Brian, " the Son of God paid earnest for this man before you bought him."

The Diabhac had to go away then.

Friar Brian asked then what would be done to him now when he had not got the man.

' I shall be put into the chamber which is for Friar Brian," said the Diabhac.[1]

" And now," said Friar Brian to the man whom he had saved, " I saved you now," says he, " and do you save me."

" What will I be able to do for you to save you ? "

" Get the axe," says Friar Brian to him, " take the head off me," says he, " and cut me up then as fine as tobacco."

He did that, and Friar Brian repented then, and he was saved.

He suffered himself to be cut as fine as tobacco on account of all he had ever done out of the way. There now, that was the end of Friar Brian.

---

[1] The meaning seems to be, that the devil who lost his quarry would suffer the same punishment as was reserved for Friar Brian.

# ST. PATRICK AND HIS GARRON

WHEN Saint Patrick came to Ireland to kindle the light of Grace in this island, many troubles were coming upon him. The island was filled with snakes, north, south, east and west, but it was God's will that Patrick should put them under foot.

When he came to West Connacht he had a servant whose name was Fintan, a pious and faithful man. One day when he was drawing towards the Reek, and the demons running away before him in fear, it chanced that Fintan was travelling in front of the saint, and the serpents came round him and killed him. When the saint came he found Fintan dead on the road. He was grieved, but he went on his knees and prayed to God to bring his servant to life again. No sooner had he his prayers finished than Fintan rose up as well as ever he was. Patrick gave thanks to God, and said, " In God's name we will set up a church here as a sign of the great power of God, and we will call it Achaidh Cobhair." [1]

The saint bought a garron or nag for carrying stones, and he blessed it ; for no burden had ever been laid upon it that it was not able to carry. Then he got workmen, masons and carpenters, and began to found the church. After a while the men began clamouring that they had nothing to eat. There was great famine and scarcity in the country that year. Meal was so scarce that few people had any to spare, or to sell, either for gold or silver.

---

[1] *i.e.*, Field of Help. This is folk etymology. Now Aughagower, in Mayo

There was a man named Black Cormac living near the place. He had the full of a barn of bags of meal. The saint took the men and the garron with him one morning to the house of Black Cormac, and he inquired how much would he be asking for as much meal as the garron would be able to carry on his back. Cormac looked at the garron and said " so much "—naming his price. " It's a bargain," said the saint, handing him money down. The men went into the barn and brought out a great bag and set it on the garron's back. Cormac said that it would break the creature's back. " Never mind," said the saint, " keep packing bags on him until I tell you to stop." They put bag after bag on him until they had a pile as big as a small house. " Drive on now," says the saint. The garron went off as readily and quickly as though it had only one bag. There was great anger on Black Cormac, and he said, " My share of trouble on ye, ye have me destroyed out and out." There was amazement upon every person who saw the garron and the load that was on him.

A short time after this the workmen asked the saint for meat, for they were working very hard. Some of them said that they heard that Black Cormac had a bull to sell cheap. The saint sent for Cormac, and asked him how much would he be wanting for the bull. Now it was a savage bull who had killed many people, and since Cormac hated the saint with a great hatred he hoped the bull would kill him, and he told him, " You can have the bull for nothing if you go yourself for him." " I'm very thankful to you," said the saint, " I'll go for him in the evening when I'll have my work done."

That evening the saint went to Black Cormac's house and asked him to show him the field where the black bull was. He was greatly delighted and said, " Follow me ; the walk is not a long one." He brought the saint down to a boreen, and showed him the bull in the field and said to him, " Take him with you now if you can." The saint went into the field, and when the bull saw him it raised its head and tail in the air and came towards him in anger. He raised his crozier and made the sign of Christ between himself and the bull. The beast lowered his head and his tail and followed the saint as quietly as a lamb.

When the saint came home he killed the bull and told the men, " Take the flesh with ye, but leave the skin and the bones." They took the flesh with them and ate it.

A week after that Black Cormac came to the saint and said, " I hear people saying that you are an honest man, but I know that you have done me a great wrong." " How so ? " said the saint. " About my meal and my bull," said he. " I gave you your own bargain for the meal, and as for your bull, you can have it back if you wish it."

" How could I get it back, and it eaten by you and your workmen ? " said Black Cormac.

The saint called for Fintan and told him, " Bring me the skin and bones of the bull." He brought them to him and he prayed over them, and in a moment the bull leapt up as well as ever he was. " Now," said the saint, " take your bull home with you."

Black Cormac was greatly surprised, and when he went home he told the neighbours that it was an enchanter the saint was, and that his own bull was a blessed bull, and that it was proper that the people should worship it. They believed that, and they said that they would come on Sunday morning.

The saint heard what Cormac had done, and he threatened him saying not to lead the people astray from the true faith that he himself was teaching them ; but Black Cormac would not listen to him. On Sunday morning some of the people gathered along with him to worship the bull, and Black Cormac was the first to go into the field to set an example, and he went to prostrate himself in presence of the bull, but the beast came and put his two horns under him behind, and tossed him up in the air so high that when he came to the ground he was dead. The people remember that, still, in West Connacht, as Cormac Dubh's Sunday.

When Saint Patrick finished his church he said Mass in it, and after that he faced for the Reek, for many of the serpents had gone up that hill out of fear of the saint. For that reason he followed them and found that they were up on the top of the Reek.

When he came to the bottom he dug a great hole, and he went up on the Reek and drove the serpents down. They fell into the hole and were all drowned but two. Those two escaped from him. One of them went into a hole in a great rock near the Mouth of the Ford[1] in Tirawley, and wrought great havoc amongst the people.

Every night when the sun would be going down this serpent used to light a candle, and anybody who would see the light used to fall dead. The people called this serpent Sercín, and the rock is to be seen to this day, and it is called Carrig-Sercín. The saint followed this serpent.

He and his servant, Fintan, came to a little village near Carrig-Sercín, and the saint asked a widow for lodgings for himself and his servant. "I'll give you that," said she, "but I must close my door before set of sun." "Why so?" said the saint. "There is a serpent in a hole of a rock out in the sea; he lights a candle every evening before sunset, and anybody who sees that light falls dead. He has great destruction made amongst the people."

---

[1] Ballina, Co. Mayo.

"Have you a candle in the house?" said the saint. "Indeed I have not," said she. "Have you the makings of a candle," said the saint. "No," said she; "but I have dry rushes."

Then the saint drew out a knife and opened Fintan's stomach and took a bit of lard out of it, and gave it to the woman of the house, and told her to make a candle. She did as he had directed, and when the candle was made the saint lit it and stood in the mouth of the door. It was not long until the serpent lit his candle, but no sooner was it lit than it fell dead. The people thanked the saint greatly, and he explained to them the mighty power and the love of God, and baptized them all.

When the other serpent escaped St. Patrick, it never stopped until it went in on a little island that was in the north of the country. The name of this serpent was Bolán Mór, or Big Bolaun. He was as big as a round tower. St. Patrick pursued Bólán; but when he came as far as the lake he had no boat to take him to the island. He stripped off his clothes, and with his crozier in his hand he leapt into the water and began swimming to the island.

When the serpent saw the saint coming to him he took to the water, and when he came as far as the saint he opened his mouth, and, as sure as I'm telling it, he swallowed the saint. Bolán Mór had a great wide stomach, and when the saint found himself shut up there he began striking on every side with his crozier, and Bólán Mór began to throw a flood of blood out of his mouth, until the water of the lake was red (dearg), and there is no name on the lake from that day to this but Loch Dearg. The saint was beating Bolán Mór with the crozier until he killed him. Then he made a hole in his side and came out, and drew Bolán Mór's body to land after him.

There was wonder and great joy on the people of the

villages round about, because neither man, beast, nor bird had come to the lake since Bólán came there but he had swallowed down into his big stomach, and it was great good for them he to be dead.

The next day the saint got a boat, and he and Fintan and a number of the people from the villages went to the island. St. Patrick blessed the little island, and it was not long until a number of pious men came and cut out [the site of] a monastery on the island, and from that time to the present, good people go on a pilgrimage to that blessed island.[1]

St. Patrick remained for a time amongst the people near Loch Derg teaching and baptising them. And as soon as some of them were able to teach the others he returned to Aughagower. While the saint had been away from them some of them had fallen into unbelief, but so soon as he came back they returned to the true faith of St. Patrick and never lost it more. Many people also came to the saint seeking to buy the little garron from him; but he would not sell it.

One day the king who was over Connacht at that time came and said, " I hear you have a wonderful garron, and that he is able to carry a heavy load."

" He is a good garron," said the saint, " no load has failed him since I bought him, and I wouldn't like to part with him."

" I'll give you as much gold as he will be able to carry on his back in one load in one day from rise of sun until it sets. It is thirty miles from my castle to this place and he must do the journey in one day."

" Perhaps you have not as much gold in the house as the garron can carry," said the saint.

" If I haven't," said the king, " I'll give you as much

---

[1] *i.e.*, Lough Derg.

as will found three churches for you, and you'll have your garron, too."

" It's a bargain," said the saint.

The king had a coach, a tent and servants, and he said, " I'll wait here till morning and you can come to my castle with me, and the morning after you can go home with your load.

" Very well, let it be so," said the saint.

On the morning of the next day they all departed, the saint riding on the garron, and the king and his servants in the coach. The king drove his horses as fast as they were able to run, to see would the garron be able to keep up with them. But if they had to go seven times as quick the garron was able for them. St. Patrick remained that night at the king's castle and next morning before sunrise the king brought himself and his garron to his treasury. The treasurer was there with his men. They filled a great bag with gold and put it on the garron's back. " Will he be able to carry it home ? " said the king. " He will, and twenty times as much," said the saint. He filled another bag and put it on him, and another bag after that. " Isn't there his enough of a load on him now ? " said the king. " There isn't a half or a quarter of a load yet on him," said the saint. They were putting [bags] on him until every ounce in the treasury was on him. Then the saint said, " To show that there isn't half a load on him yet, put two or three tons of iron on top of the gold." They did that, and the garron walked out as lightly as though there had been nothing in it but a bag of oats. " Now," said the saint, " you see that my garron-*een* hasn't half a load on him yet." " I see he has not," said the king. " There is more power in your garron than in all the horses of the Ard-ri.[1] Take your garron home

---

[1] *i.e.*, The High King.

again, and begin and set up those churches, and I'll pay the cost."

The saint rode on his garron and came home. He soon began to put up the three churches, and the king paid the costs. But the garron carried every stone that went to the building. The people have the old saying still when they want to praise anyone, " May you have the strength of Patrick's garron ! "

When the three churches were finished he bestowed his garron on the brethren, and he himself went northward, lighting a coal of faith throughout Ireland which was never quenched, and never shall be quenched.

When the great judgment shall come it is St. Patrick who will judge the children of the Gael.

# TEIG O'KANE (TADHG O CÁTHAIN) AND THE CORPSE

THERE was once a grown-up lad in the County Leitrim, and he was strong and lively, and the son of a rich farmer. His father had plenty of money, and he did not spare it on the son. Accordingly, when the boy grew up he liked sport better than work, and, as his father had no other children, he loved this one so much that he allowed him to do in everything just as it pleased himself. He was very extravagant, and he used to scatter the gold money as another person would scatter the white. He was seldom to be found at home, but if there was a fair, or a race, or a gathering within ten miles of him, you were dead certain to find him there. And he seldom spent a night in his father's house, but he used to be always out rambling, and, like Shawn Bwee long ago, there was

"grádh gach cailín i mbrollach a léine,"

"the love of every girl in the breast of his shirt," and it's many's the kiss he got and he gave, for he was very handsome, and there wasn't a girl in the country but would fall in love with him, only for him to fasten his two eyes on her, and it was for that someone made this rann on him—

"Feuch an rógaire 'g iarraidh póige,
  Ni h-iongantas mór é a bheith mar atá
Ag leanamhaint a gcómhnuidhe d'arnán na graineoige
  Anuas 's aníos 's nna chodladh 'sa lá."

"Look at the rogue, it's for kisses he's rambling,
  It isn't much wonder, for that was his way;
He's like an old hedgehog, at night he'll be scrambling
  From this place to that, but he'll sleep in the day."

At last he became very wild and unruly. He wasn't to be seen day nor night in his father's house, but always rambling or going on his kailee (night-visit) from place to place and from house to house, so that the old people used to shake their heads and say to one another, " it's easy seen what will happen to the land when the old man dies ; his son will run through it in a year, and it won't stand him that long itself."

He used to be always gambling and card-playing and drinking, but his father never minded his bad habits, and never punished him. But it happened one day that the old man was told that the son had ruined the character of a girl in the neighbourhood, and he was greatly angry, and he called the son to him, and said to him, quietly and sensibly—" Avic," says he, " you know I loved you greatly up to this, and I never stopped you from doing your choice thing whatever it was, and I kept plenty of money with you, and I always hoped to leave you the house and land and all I had, after myself would be gone ; but I heard a story of you to-day that has disgusted me with you. I cannot tell you the grief that I felt when I heard such a thing of you, and I tell you now plainly that unless you marry that girl I'll leave house and land and everything to my brother's son. I never could leave it to anyone who would make so bad a use of it as you do yourself, deceiving women and coaxing girls. Settle with yourself now whether you'll marry that girl and get my land as a fortune with her, or refuse to marry her and give up all that was coming to you ; and tell me in the morning which of the two things you have chosen."

" Och ! murdher sheery ! father, you wouldn't say that to me, and I such a good son as I am. Who told you I wouldn't marry the girl ? " says he.

But the father was gone, and the lad knew well enough that he would keep his word too ; and he was greatly troubled in his mind, for as quiet and as kind as the father was, he never went back of a word that he had once said, and there wasn't another man in the country who was harder to bend that he was.

The boy did not know rightly what to do. He was in love with the girl indeed, and he hoped to marry her some time or other, but he would much sooner have remained another while as he was, and follow on at his old tricks—drinking, sporting, and playing cards; and, along with that, he was angry that his father should order him to marry and should threaten him if he did not do it.

"Isn't my father a great fool," says he to himself. "I was ready enough, and only too anxious, to marry Mary; and now since he threatened me, faith I've a great mind to let it go another while."

His mind was so much excited that he remained between two notions as to what he should do. He walked out into the night at last to cool his heated blood, and went on to the road. He lit a pipe, and as the night was fine he walked and walked on, until the quick pace made him begin to forget his trouble. The night was bright and the moon half full. There was not a breath of wind blowing, and the air was calm and mild. He walked on for nearly three hours, when he suddenly remembered that it was late in the night, and time for him to turn. "Musha! I think I forgot myself," says he; "it must be near twelve o'clock now."

The word was hardly out of his mouth when he heard the sound of many voices and the trampling of feet on the road before him. "I don't know who can be out so late at night as this, and on such a lonely road," said he to himself.

He stood listening and he heard the voices of many people talking through other, but he could not understand what they were saying. "Oh, wirra!" says he, "I'm afraid. It's not Irish or English they have; it can't be they're Frenchmen!" He went on a couple of yards further, and he saw well enough by the light of the moon a band of little people coming towards him, and they were carrying something big and heavy with them. " Oh, murdher!" says he to himself, "sure it can't be that they're the good people that's in it!" Every rib of hair that was on his head stood up, and there fell a shaking on his bones, for he saw that they were coming to him fast.

He looked at them again, and perceived that there were about twenty little men in it, and there was not a man at all of them higher than about three feet or three feet and a half, and some of them were grey, and seemed very old. He looked again, but he could not make out what was the heavy thing they were carrying until they came up to him, and then they all stood round about him. They threw the heavy thing down on the road, and he saw on the spot that it was a dead body.

He became as cold as the Death, and there was not a drop of blood running in his veins when an old little grey man*een* came up to him and said, " Isn't it lucky we met you, Teig O'Kane ? "

Poor Teig could not bring out a word at all, nor open his lips, if he were to get the world for it, and so he gave no answer.

" Teig O'Kane," said the little grey man again, " isn't it timely you met us ? "

Teig could not answer him.

" Teig O'Kane," says he, " the third time, isn't it lucky and timely that we met you ? "

But Teig remained silent, for he was afraid to return an answer, and his tongue was as if it was tied to the roof of his mouth.

The little grey man turned to his companions, and there was joy in his bright little eye. " And now," says he, " Teig O'Kane hasn't a word, we can do with him what we please. Teig, Teig," says he, " you're living a bad life, and we can make a slave of you now, and you cannot withstand us, for there's no use in trying to go against us. Lift that corpse."

Teig was so frightened that he was only able to utter the two words, " I won't ; " for as frightened as he was, he was obstinate and stiff, the same as ever.

" Teig O'Kane won't lift the corpse," said the little man*een*, with a wicked little laugh, for all the world like the breaking of a lock of dry kippeens, and with a little harsh voice like the striking of a cracked bell. " Teig O'Kane won't lift the corpse—make him lift it ; " and before the word was out of his mouth they had all gathered round poor Teig, and they all talking and laughing through other.

Teig tried to run from them, but they followed him, and a man of them stretched out his foot before him as he ran, so that Teig was thrown in a heap on the road. Then before he could rise up, the fairies caught him, some by the hands and some by the feet, and they held him tight, in a way that he could not stir, with his face against the ground. Six or seven of them raised the body then, and pulled it over to him, and left it down on his back. The breast of the corpse was squeezed against Teig's back and shoulders, and the arms of the corpse were thrown around Teig's neck. Then they stood back from him a couple of yards, and let him get up. He rose, foaming at the mouth and cursing, and he shook himself, thinking to throw the corpse off his back. But his fear and his wonder were great when he found that the two arms had a tight hold round his own neck, and that the two legs were squeezing his hips firmly, and that, however strongly he tried, he could not throw it off, any more than a horse can throw off its saddle. He was terribly frightened then, and he thought he was lost. " Ochone ! for ever," said he to himself, " it's the bad life I'm leading that has given the good people this power over me    I promise to God and Mary, Peter and Paul, Patrick and Bridget, that I'll mend my ways for as long as I have to live, if I come clear out of this danger—and I'll marry the girl."

The little grey man came up to him again, and said he to him, " Now, Teig*een*," says he, " you didn't lift the body when I told you to lift it, and see how you were made to lift it ; perhaps when I tell you to bury it you won't bury it until you're made to bury it ! "

" Anything at all that I can do for your honour," said Teig, " I'll do it," for he was getting sense already, and if it had not been for the great fear that was on him, he never would have let that civil word slip out of his mouth.

The little man laughed a sort of laugh again. " You're getting quiet now, Teig," says he. " I'll go bail but you'll be quiet enough before I'm done with you. Listen to me now, Teig O'Kane, and if you don't obey me in all I'm telling you to do, you'll repent it. You must carry with you this corpse that is on your back to Teampoll-Démuis, and you must bring it into the church with you, and make a grave for it in the very middle of the church, and you must raise up the flags and put them down again the very same way, and you must carry the clay out of the church and leave the place as it was when you came, so that no one could know that there had been anything changed. But that's not all. Maybe that the body won't be allowed to be buried in that church ; perhaps some other man has the bed, and, if so, it's likely he won't share it with this one. If you don't get leave to bury it in Teampoll-Démuis, you must carry it to Carrick-fhad-vic-Oruis, and bury it in the churchyard there ; and if you don't get it into that place, take it with you to Teampoll-Ronáin ; and if that churchyard is closed on you, take it to Imlogue-Fhada; and if you're not able to bury it there, you've no more to do than to take it to Kill-

Breedya, and you can bury it there without hindrance. I cannot tell you what one of those churches is the one where you will have leave to bury that corpse under the clay, but I know that it will be allowed you to bury him at some church or other of them. If you do this work rightly, we will be thankful to you, and you will have no cause to grieve; but if you are slow or lazy, believe me we shall take satisfaction of you."

When the grey little man had done speaking, his comrades laughed and clapped their hands together. "Glic! Glic! Hwee! Hwee!" they all cried; "go on, go on, you have eight hours before you till daybreak, and if you haven't this man buried before the sun rises, you're lost." They struck a fist and a foot behind on him, and drove him on in the road. He was obliged to walk, and to walk fast, for they gave him no rest.

He thought himself that there was not a wet path, or a dirty boreen, or a crooked contrary road in the whole county that he had not walked that night. The night was at times very dark, and whenever there would come a cloud across the moon he could see nothing, and then he used often to fall. Sometimes he was hurt, and sometimes he escaped, but he was obliged always to rise on the moment and to hurry on. Sometimes the moon would break out clearly, and then he would look behind him and see the little people following at his back. And he heard them speaking amongst themselves, talking and crying out, and screaming like a flock of sea-gulls; and if he was to save his soul he never understood as much as one word of what they were saying.

He did not know how far he had walked, when at last one of them cried out to him, "Stop here!" He stood, and they all gathered round him.

"Do you see those withered trees over there?" says the old boy to him again. "Teampoll-Démuis is among those trees, and you must go in there by yourself, for we cannot follow you or go with you. We must remain here. Go on boldly."

Teig looked from him, and he saw a high wall that was in places half broken down, and an old grey church on the inside of the wall, and about a dozen withered old trees scattered here and there round it. There was neither leaf nor twig on any of them, but their bare crooked branches were stretched out like the arms of an angry man when he threatens. He had no help for it, but was obliged to go forward. He was a couple of hundred yards from the church, but he walked on, and never looked behind him until he came to the gate of the churchyard. The old gate was thrown down, and he had no difficulty in entering. He turned then to see if any of the little people were following him, but there came a cloud over the moon, and the night became so dark that he could see nothing. He went into the churchyard, and he walked up the old grassy pathway leading to the church. When he reached the door, he found it locked. The door was large and strong, and he did not know what to do. At last he drew out his knife with difficulty, and stuck it in the wood to try if it were not rotten, but it was not.

"Now," said he to himself, "I have no more to do; the door is shut, and I can't open it."

Before the words were rightly shaped in his own mind, a voice in his ear said to him, "Search for the key on the top of the door, or on the wall."

He started. "Who is that speaking to me?" he cried, turning round; but he saw no one. The voice said in his ear again, "Search for the key on the top of the door, or on the wall."

"What's that?" said he, and the sweat running from his forehead; "who spoke to me?"

"It's I, the corpse, that spoke to you!" said the voice.

"Can you talk?" said Teig.

"Now and again," said the corpse.

Teig searched for the key, and he found it on the top of the wall. He was too much frightened to say any more, but he opened the door wide, and as quickly as he could, and he went in, with the corpse on his back. It was as dark as pitch inside, and poor Teig began to shake and tremble.

"Light the candle," said the corpse.

Teig put his hand in his pocket, as well as he was able, and drew out a flint and steel. He struck a spark out of it, and lit a burnt rag he had in his pocket. He blew it until it made a flame, and he looked round him. The church was very ancient, and part of the wall was broken down. The windows were blown in or cracked, and the timber of the seats was rotten. There were six or seven old iron candlesticks left there still, and in one of these candlesticks Teig found the stump of an old candle, and he lit it. He was still looking round him on the strange and horrid place in which he found himself, when the cold corpse whispered in his ear, "Bury me now, bury me now; there is a spade and turn the ground." Teig looked from him, and he saw a spade lying beside the altar. He took it up, and he placed the blade under a flag that was in the middle of the aisle, and leaning all his weight on the handle of the spade, he raised it. When the first flag was raised it was not hard to raise the others near it, and he moved three or four of them out of their places. The clay that was under them was soft and easy to dig, but he had not thrown up more than three or four shovelfuls, when he felt the iron touch something soft like flesh. He threw up three or four more shovelfuls from around it, and then he saw that it was another body that was buried in the same place.

"I am afraid I'll never be allowed to bury the two

bodies in the same hole," said Teig, in his own mind. "You corpse, there on my back," says he, "will you be satisfied if I bury you down here?" But the corpse never answered him a word.

"That's a good sign," said Teig to himself. "Maybe he's getting quiet," and he thrust the spade down in the earth again. Perhaps he hurt the flesh of the other body, for the dead man that was buried there stood up in the grave, and shouted an awful shout. "Hoo! hoo!! hoo!!! Go! go!! go!!! or you're a dead, dead, dead man!" And then he fell back in the grave again. Teig said afterwards, that of all the wonderful things he saw that night, that was the most awful to him. His hair stood upright on his head like the bristles of a pig, the cold sweat ran off his face, and then came a tremor over all his bones, until he thought that he must fall.

But after a while he became bolder, when he saw that the second corpse remained lying quietly there, and he threw in the clay on it again, and he smoothed it overhead, and he laid down the flags carefully as they had been before. "It can't be that he'll rise up any more," said he.

He went down the aisle a little further, and drew near to the door, and began raising the flags again, looking for another bed for the corpse on his back. He took up three or four flags and put them aside, and then he dug the clay. He was not long digging until he laid bare an old woman without a thread upon her but her shirt. She was more lively than the first corpse, for he had scarcely taken any of the clay away from about her, when she sat up and began to cry, "Ho, you bodach (clown)! Ha, you bodach! Where has he been that he got no bed?"

Poor Teig drew back, and when she found that she was getting no answer, she closed her eyes gently, lost her vigour, and fell back quietly and slowly under the clay.

Teig did to her as he had done to the man—he threw the clay back on her, and left the flags down overhead.

He began digging again near the door, but before he had thrown up more than a couple of shovelfuls, he noticed a man's hand laid bare by the spade. "By my soul, I'll go no further, then," said he to himself; "what use is it for me?" And he threw the clay in again on it, and settled the flags as they had been before.

He left the church then, and his heart was heavy enough, but he shut the door and locked it, and left the key where he found it. He sat down on a tombstone that was near the door, and began thinking. He was in great doubt what he should do. He laid his face between his two hands, and cried for grief and fatigue, since he was dead certain at this time that he never would come home alive. He made another attempt to loosen the hands of the corpse that were squeezed round his neck, but they were as tight as if they were clamped; and the more he tried to loosen them, the tighter they squeezed him. He was going to sit down once more, when the cold, horrid lips of the dead man said to him, "Carrick-fhad-vic-Oruis," and he remembered the command of the good people to bring the corpse with him to that place if he should be unable to bury it where he had been

He rose up and looked about him. "I don't know the way," he said.

As soon as he had uttered the words, the corpse stretched out suddenly its left hand that had been tightened round his neck, and kept it pointing out, showing, him the road he ought to follow. Teig went in the direction that the fingers were stretched, and passed out of the churchyard. He found himself on an old rutty, stony road, and he stood still again, not knowing where to turn. The corpse stretched out its bony hand a second time, and pointed out to him another road—not the road by which he had come when approaching the old church. Teig followed that road, and whenever he came to a path or road meeting it, the corpse always stretched out its hand and pointed with its fingers, showing him the way he was to take.

Many was the cross-road he turned down, and many was the crooked boreen he walked, until he saw from him an old burying-ground at last, beside the road, but there was neither church nor chapel nor any other building in it. The corpse squeezed him tightly, and he stood. " Bury me, bury me in the burying-ground," said the voice.

Teig drew over towards the old burying-place, and he was not more than about twenty yards from it, when, raising his eyes, he saw hundreds and hundreds of ghosts—men, women, and children—sitting on the top of the wall round about, or standing on the inside of it, or running backwards and forwards, and pointing at him, while he could see their mouths opening and shutting as if they were speaking, though he heard no word, nor any sound amongst them at all.

He was afraid to go forward, so he stood where he was, and the moment he stood, all the ghosts became quiet, and ceased moving. Then Teig understood that it was trying to keep him from going in that they were. He walked a couple of yards forwards, and immediately the whole crowd rushed together towards the spot to which he was moving, and they stood so thickly together that it seemed to him that he never could break through them, even though he had a mind to try. But he had no mind to try it. He went back broken and disspirited, and when he had gone a couple of hundred yards from the burying-ground, he stood again, for he did not know what way he was to go. He heard the voice of the corpse in his ear, saying " Teampoll-Ronáin," and the skinny hand was stretched out again, pointing him out the road.

As tired as he was, he had to walk, and the road was neither short nor even. The night was darker than ever, and it was difficult to make his way. Many was the toss he got, and many a bruise they left on his body. At last he saw Teampoll-Ronáin from him in the distance, standing in the middle of the burying-ground. He moved over towards it, and thought he was all right and safe, when he saw no ghosts nor anything else on the wall, and he thought he would never be hindered now from leaving his load off him at last. He moved over to the gate, but as he was passing in, he tripped on the threshold. Before he could recover himself, something that he could not see seized him by the neck, by the hands, and by the feet, and bruised him, and shook him up, and choked him, until he was nearly dead; and at last he was lifted up, and carried more than a hundred yards from that place, and then thrown down in an old dyke, with the corpse still clinging to him.

He rose up, bruised and sore, but feared to go near the place again, for he had seen nothing the time he was thrown down and carried away

"You, corpse up on my back," said he, "shall I go over again to the churchyard?"—but the corpse never answered him. "That's a sign you don't wish me to try it again," said Teig.

He was now in great doubt as to what he ought to do, when the corpse spoke in his ear, and said "Imlogue-Fhada."

"Oh, murder!" said Teig, "must I bring you there? If you keep me long walking like this, I tell you I'll fall under you."

He went on, however, in the direction the corpse pointed out to him. He could not have told, himself, how long he had been going, when the dead man behind suddenly squeezed him, and said, "There!"

Teig looked from him, and he saw a little low wall, that was so broken down in places that it was no wall at all. It was in a great wide field, in from the road; and only for three or four great stones at the corners, that were more like rocks than stones, there was nothing to show that there was either graveyard or burying-ground there.

"Is this Imlogue-Fhada? Shall I bury you here?" said Teig.

"Yes," said the voice.

"But I see no grave or gravestone, only this pile of stones," said Teig.

The corpse did not answer, but stretched out its long fleshless hand, to show Teig the direction in which he was to go. Teig went on accordingly, but he was greatly terrified, for he remembered what had happened to him at the last place. He went on, "with his heart in his mouth," as he said himself afterwards; but when he came to within fifteen or twenty yards of the little low square wall, there broke out a flash of lightning, bright yellow and red, with blue streaks in it, and went round about the wall in one course, and it swept by as fast as the swallow in the clouds, and the longer Teig remained looking at it the faster it went, till at last it became like a bright ring of flame round the old graveyard, which no one could pass without being burnt by it. Teig never saw, from the time he was born, and never saw afterwards, so wonderful or so splendid a sight as that was. Round went the flame, white and yellow and blue sparks leaping out from it as it went, and although at first it had been no more than a thin, narrow line, it increased slowly until it was at last a great broad band, and it was continually getting broader and higher, and throwing out more brilliant sparks, till there was never a colour on the ridge of the earth that was not to be seen in that fire; and lightning never shone and flame never flamed that was so shining and so bright as that.

Teig was amazed; he was half dead with fatigue, and he had no courage left to approach the wall. There fell a mist over his eyes, and there came a soorawn in his head, and he was obliged to sit down upon a great stone to recover himself. He could see nothing but the light, and he could hear nothing but the whirr of it as it shot round the paddock faster than a flash of lightning.

As he sat there on the stone, the voice whispered once more in his ear, " Kill-Breedya "; and the dead man squeezed him so tightly that he cried out. He rose again, sick, tired, and trembling, and went forwards as he was directed. The wind was cold, and the road was bad, and the load upon his back was heavy, and the night was dark, and he himself was nearly worn out, and if he had had very much farther to go he must have fallen dead under his burden.

At last the corpse stretched out its hand, and said to him, " Bury me there."

" This is the last burying-place," said Teig in his own mind; " and the little grey man said I'd be allowed to bury him in some of them, so it must be this; it can't be but they'll let him in here."

The first faint streak of the ring of day was appearing in the east, and the clouds were beginning to catch fire, but it was darker than ever, for the moon was set, and there were no stars.

" Make haste, make haste ! " said the corpse; and Teig hurried forward as well as he could to the graveyard, which was a little place on a bare hill, with only a few graves in it. He walked boldly in through the open gate, and nothing touched him, nor did he either hear or see anything. He came to the middle of the ground, and then stood up and looked round him for a spade or shovel to make a grave. As he was turning round and searching, he suddenly perceived what startled him greatly—a newly-dug grave right before him. He moved over to it, and looked down, and there at the bottom he saw a black coffin. He clambered down into the hole and lifted the lid, and found that (as he thought it would be) the coffin was empty. He had hardly mounted up out of the hole, and was standing on the brink, when the corpse, which had clung to him for more than eight hours, suddenly relaxed its hold of his neck, and loosened its shins from round his hips, and sank down with a plop into the open coffin.

Teig fell down on his two knees at the brink of the grave, and gave thanks to God. He made no delay then, but pressed down the coffin lid in its place, and threw in the clay over it with his two hands; and when the grave was filled up, he stamped and leaped on it with his feet, until it was firm and hard, and then he left the place.

The sun was fast rising as he finished his work, and the first thing he did was to return to the road, and look out for a house to rest himself in. He found an inn at last, and lay down upon a bed there, and slept till night. Then he rose up and ate a little, and fell asleep again till morning. When he awoke in the morning he hired a horse and rode home. He was more than twenty-six miles from home where he was, and he had come all that way with the dead body on his back in one night.

All the people at his own home thought that he must have left the country, and they rejoiced greatly when they saw him come back. Everyone began asking him where he had been, but he would not tell anyone except his father.

He was a changed man from that day. He never drank too much; he never lost his money over cards; and especially he would not take the world and be out late by himself of a dark night.

He was not a fortnight at home until he married Mary, the girl he had been in love with; and it's at their wedding the sport was, and it's he was the happy man from that day forward, and it's all I wish that we may be as happy as he was.

# THE BUIDEACH, THE TINKER, AND THE BLACK DONKEY

In times long ago there was a poor widow living near Castlebar, in the County Mayo. She had an only son, and he never grew one inch from the time he was five years old, and the people called him Buídeach[1] as a nick-name.

One day when the Buideach was about fifteen years of age his mother went to Castlebar. She was not gone more than an hour when there came a big Tinker, and a Black Donkey with him, to the door, and "Are you in, woman of the house?" said the tinker.

"She is not," said the Buideach, "and she told me not to let anyone in until she'd come home herself."

The Tinker walked in, and when he looked at the Buideach he said, "Indeed you're a nice boy to keep anyone at all out, you could not keep out a turkey cock."

The Buideach rose of a leap and gave the big Tinker a fist between the two eyes and pitched him out on the top of his head, under the feet of the Black Donkey.

The Tinker rose up in a rage and made an attempt to get hold of the Buideach, but he gave him another fist at the butt of the ear and threw him out again under the feet of the Black Donkey.

The donkey began to bray pitifully, and when the Buideach went out to see [why], the Tinker was dead. "You have killed my master," said the Black Donkey, "and indeed I am not sorry for it, he often gave me a heavy beating without cause."

---

[1] Or better, Buighdeach, pronounced Bweed-yach, *i.e.*, Bweed-ya with a guttural *ch* (as in lo*ch*) at the end.

The Buideach was astonished when he heard the Black Donkey speaking, and he said, "You are not a proper donkey."

"Indeed, I have only been an ass for seven years. My story is a pitiful one. I was the son of a gentleman."

"Musha, then, I would like to hear your story," said the Buideach.

"Come in, then, to the end of the house. Cover up the Tinker in the dunghill, and I will tell you my story."

The Buideach drew the dead man over to the dunghill and covered him up. The Black Donkey walked into the house and said, " I was the son of a gentleman, but I was a bad son, and I died under a heavy load of deadly sins on my poor soul; and I would be burning in hell now were it not for the Virgin Mary. I used to say a little prayer in honour of her every night, and when I went into the presence of the Great Judge I was sentenced to hell until His mother spoke to the Judge and He changed his sentence, and there was made of me a Black Donkey, and I was given to the Tinker for the space of seven years, until he should die a worldly [or corporeal] death. The Tinker was a limb of the devil, and it was I who gave you strength to kill him; but you are not done with him yet. He will come to life again at the end of seven days, and if you are there before him he will kill you as sure as you are alive."

"I never left this townland since I was born," said the Buideach, "and I would not like to desert my mother."

"Would it not be better for you to leave your mother than to lose your life in a state of mortal sin and be for ever burning in hell?"

"I don't know any place where I could go into hiding," said the Buideach; "but since it has turned out that it was you who put strength into my hand to kill the Tinker, perhaps you would direct me to some place where

I could be safe from him."

"Did you ever hear talk of Lough Derg?"

"Indeed, I did," said the Buideach; "my grandmother was once on a pilgrimage there, but I don't know where it is."

"I will bring you there to-morrow night. There is a monastery underground on the island, and an old friar in it who sees the Virgin Mary every Saturday. Tell him your case and take his advice in every single thing. He will put you to penance, but penance on this world is better than the pains of hell for ever. You know where the little dún[1] is, which is at the back of the old castle. If you are in the dún about three hours after nightfall I shall be there before you and bring you to Lough Derg.

"I shall be there if I'm alive," said the Buideach; "but is there any fear of me that the Tinker will get up before that time?"

"There is no fear," said the Black Donkey, "unless you tell somebody that you killed him. If you tell anything about him he will get up and he will slay yourself and your mother."

"By my soul, then, I'll be silent about him," said the Buideach.

That evening when the Buideach's mother came home she asked him did anybody come to the house since she went away.

"I did not see anyone," said he, "but an old pedlar with a bag, and he got nothing from me."

"I see the track of the shoe of a horse or a donkey outside the door, and it was not there in the morning when I was going out," said she.

"It was Páidin Éamoinn the fool, who was riding

---

[1] Literally, "fort," pronounced like "dhoon." Usually a half-levelled earthen rampart.

Big Mary O'Brien's ass," said the Buideach.

The Buideach never slept a wink all that night but thinking of the Tinker and the Black Donkey. The next day he was in great anxiety. His mother observed that and asked him what was on him.

"There's not a feather on me," says he.

That night when the mother was asleep the Buideach stole out and never stopped until he came to the little dún; the Black Donkey was there before him and said, "Are you ready?"

"I am," said the Buideach, "but I am grieved that I did not get my mother's blessing; she will be very anxious until I come back again."

"Indeed she will not be anxious at all, because there is another Buideach at your mother's side at home, so like you that she won't know that it is not yourself that's in it; but I'll bring him away with me before you come back."

"I am very much obliged to you and I am ready to go with you now," said he.

"Leap up on my back; there is a long journey before us," said the Donkey.

The Buideach leapt on his back, and the moment he did so he heard thunder and saw great lightning. There came down a big cloud which closed around the black ass and its rider. The Buideach lost the sight of his eyes, and a heavy sleep fell upon him, and when he awoke he was on an island in Lough Derg, standing in the presence of the ancient friar.

The friar began to talk to him, and said, "What brought you here, my son?"

"Well, then, indeed, I don't rightly know," said the Buideach.

"I will know soon," said the friar; "come with me."

He followed the old friar down under the earth, until they came to a little chamber that was cut in the rock. "Now," said the friar, "go down on your knees and make your confession and do not conceal any crime."

The Buideach went down on his knees and told everything that happened to him concerning the Tinker and the Black Donkey.

The friar then put him under penance for seven days and seven nights, without food or drink, walking on his bare knees amongst the rocks and sharp stones. He went through the penance, and by the seventh day there was not a morsel of skin or flesh on his knees, and he was like a shadow with the hunger. When he had the penance finished the old friar came and said, "It's time for you to be going home."

"I have no knowledge of the way or of how to go back," said the Buideach.

"Your friend the Black Donkey will bring you back," said the friar. "He will be here to-night; and when you go home spend your life piously and do not tell to anyone except to your father-confessor that yo were here."

"Tell me, father, is there any danger of me from the Tinker?"

"There is not," said the friar; "he is an ass [himself now] with a tinker from the province of Munster, and he will be in that shape for one and twenty years, and after that he will go to eternal rest. Depart now to your chamber. You will hear a little bell after the darkness of night [has fallen], and as soon as you shall hear it, go up on to the island, and the Black Donkey will be there before you, and he will bring you home; my blessing with you."

The Buideach went to his room, and as soon as he heard

the bell he went up to the island and his friend the Black Donkey was waiting for him.

" Jump up on my back, Buideach, I have not a moment to lose," said the donkey.

He did so, and on the spot he heard the thunder and saw the lightning. A great cloud came down and enveloped the Black Donkey and its rider. Heavy sleep fell upon the Buideach, and when he awoke he found himself in the little dún at home standing in the presence of the Black Donkey.

" Go home now to your mother. The other Buideach is gone from her side ; she is in deep sleep and she won't feel you going in."

" Is there any fear of me from the Tinker ? " said he.

" Did not the blessed friar tell you that there is not," said the Black Donkey. " I will protect you. Put your hand in my left ear, and you will get there a purse which will, never be empty during your life. Be good to poor people and to widows and to orphans, and you will have a long life and a happy death, and heaven at the end."

The Buideach went home and went to sleep, and the mother never had had a notion that the other Buideach was not her own son.

At the end of a week after this the Buideach said to his mother, " Is not this a fair day in Castlebar ? "

" Yes, indeed," said she.

" Well then, you ought to go there and buy a cow," says he.

" Don't be humbugging your mother or you'll have no luck," says she.

" Upon my word I am not humbugging," said he. " God sent a purse my way, and there is more than the price of a cow in it."

"Perhaps you did not get it honestly; tell me where did you find it?"

"I'll tell you nothing about it, except that I found it honestly, and if you have any doubt about my word, let the thing be."

Women are nearly always given to covetousness, and she was not free from it.

"Give me the price of the cow."

He handed her twenty pieces of gold. "You'll get a good cow for all that money," said he.

"I will," said she, "but I'd like to have the price of a pig."

"Do not be greedy, mother," said he; "you won't get any more this time."

The mother went to the fair and she bought a milch cow, and some clothes for the Buideach, and when he got her gone he went to the parish priest and said that he would like to make confession. He told the priest then everything that happened to him from the time he met the Tinker and the Black Donkey.

"Indeed, you are a good boy," said the priest, "give me some of the gold."

The Buideach, gave him twenty pieces, but he was not satisfied with that, and he asked for the price of a horse.

"I did not think that a priest would be covetous," said he, "but I see now that they are as covetous as women. Here are twenty more pieces for you; are you satisfied now?"

"I am, and I am not," said the priest. "Since you have a purse which will never be empty as long as you live, you should be able to give me as much as would set up a fine church in place of the miserable one which we have in the parish now."

"Get workmen and masons, and begin the church, and I'll give you the workmen's wages from week to week," said the Buideach.

"I'd sooner have it now," said the priest. "A thousand pieces will do the work, and if you give them to me now I'll put up the church."

The Buideach gave him one thousand pieces of gold out of the purse, and the purse was none the lighter for it.

The Buideach came home and his mother was there before him, with a fine milch cow and new clothes for himself. "Indeed, that's a good cow," said he; "we can give the poor people some milk every morning."

"Indeed they must wait until I churn, and I'll give them the buttermilk—until I buy a pig."

"It's the new milk you'll give the poor people," said the Buideach, "we can buy butter."

"I think you have lost your senses," says the mother. "You'll want the little share of riches which God sent you before I'm a year in the grave."

"How do you know but that I might not be in the grave before you?" said he; "but at all events God will send me my enough."

When they were talking there came a poor woman, and three children to the door and asked for alms in the honour of God and Mary.

"I have nothing for ye this time," said the widow.

"Don't say that, mother," said the Buideach. "I have alms to give in the name of God and His mother Mary." With that he went out and gave a gold piece to the poor woman, and said to his mother, "Milk the cow and give those poor children a drink."

"I will not," said the mother.

"Then I'll do it myself," said he.

He got the vessel, milked the cow, and gave lots of new milk to the poor children and to the woman. When they were gone away the mother said to him, "Your purse will be soon empty."

"I have no fear of that," said he; "it's God who sent

it to me, and I'll make a good use of it," says he.

"Have your own way,"[1] said she; "but you'll be sorry for it yet."

The next day lots of people came to the Buideach asking for alms, and he never let them go away from him empty-[handed]. The name and fame of the Buideach went through the country like lightning and men said that he was in partnership with the good people [*i.e.* fairies]. But others said that it was the devil who was giving him the gold, and they made a complaint against him to the parish priest. But the priest said that the Buideach was a decent good boy, and that it was God who gave him the means, and that he was making good use of them.

The Buideach went on well now, and he began growing until he was almost six feet high.

His mother died and he fell in love with a pretty girl, and he was not long until they were married.

He had not a day's luck from that time forward. His wife got to know that he had a wonderful purse and nothing could satisfy her but she must get it. He refused her often, but she was giving him no rest, day or night, until she got the purse from him at last. Then, when she got it, she had no respect for it. She went to Castlebar to buy silks and satins, but when she opened the purse in place of gold pieces being in it there was nothing but pieces of pebbles. She came back and great anger on her; and said, "Isn't it a nice fool you made of me giving me a purse filled with little stones instead of the purse with the gold in it."

"I gave you the right purse," said he; "I have no second one."

He seized the purse and opened it, and as sure as I'm

---

[1] Literally, "do you our will."

telling it to you, there was nothing in it but little bits of pebbles.

There was an awful grief upon the Buideach, and it was not long until he was mad, tearing his hair, and beating his head against the wall.

The priest was sent for but he could get neither sense nor reason out of the Buideach. He tore off his clothes and went naked and mad through the country.

About a week after that the neighbours found the poor Buideach dead at the foot of a bush in the little dún.

That old bush is growing in the dún yet, and the people call it the " Buideach's Bush," but [as for himself] it is certain that he went to heaven.

# GOD SPARE YOU YOUR HEALTH

THERE was a smith in Skibbereen long ago, long before the foreigners nested there, and people used to be coming to him who did not please him too well. When he would do some little turn of work for them in the forge they used only have a " God spare you your health " for him. It's a very nice prayer, " God spare you your health," but when the smith used to go out to buy bread he used not to get it without money. Prayers, no matter how good, would not do the business for him. He used often to be half mad with them, but he used not to say anything. He was so vexed with that work one day that he took a hound he had from his house into his forge, and he tied it there with a wisp of hay under it. " Yes," said he, " we will soon see whether the prayers of these poor people will feed my hound."

The first person who came and had nothing but a "God spare you the health" in place of payment. "Right," said the smith, " let my hound have that."

Other people came to the forge, and they without any payment for the poor smith but that same fine prayer, and according as the smith used to get the prayers he used to bestow them on the hound. He used to give it no other food or drink. The prayers were the hound's food, but they made poor meat for him, for the smith found him dead in the morning after his being dependent on the feeding of the prayers.

A man came to the forge that day and he had a couple of hinges and a couple of reaping hooks, that were not too strong, to be fixed. The smith did the work, and the man was thinking of going, " God spare you the health," said he. Instead of the answer " Amen ! Lord ! and you likewise " ; what the smith did was to take the man by the shoulder. " Look over in the corner," said he ; " my hound is dead, and if prayers could feed it, it ought to be fat and strong. I have given every prayer I got this while back to that hound there, but they have not done the business for it. And it's harder to feed a man than a hound. Do you understand, my good man ? "

He did apparently, for he put his hand in his pocket. " What's the cost ? " said he.

It was short until all the neighbours heard talk of the death of that hound of the smith's, and much oftener from that out used their tune to be, " What's the cost, Dermot ? " than " God spare you your health."

# SAINT PETER

AT the time that St. Peter and our Saviour were walking the country, many was the marvel that his Master showed him, and if it had been another person who was in it and who had seen half as much, no doubt his confidence in his Master would have been stronger than that of Peter.

One day they were entering a town, and there was a musician sitting half-drunk on the side of the road and he asking for alms. Our Saviour gave him a piece of money, going by of him. There came wonder on Peter at that, for he said to himself, " many's the poor man in great want that my Master refused, but now He has given alms to this drunken musician; but perhaps," says he to himself, " perhaps He likes music."

Our Saviour knew what was in Peter's mind, but he did not speak a word about it.

On the next day they were journeying again, and a poor friar (*sic*) met them, and he bowed down with age and almost naked. He asked our Saviour for alms, but He took no notice of him, and did not answer his request.

" There's another thing that's not right," said Peter in his own mind. He was afraid to speak to his Master about it, but he was losing his confidence in Him every day.

The same evening they were approaching another village when a blind man met them and he asking alms. Our Saviour talked with him and said, " What do you want ? " " The price of a night's lodging, the price of something to eat, and as much as I shall want to-morrow: if you can give it to me you shall get great recompense, and recompense that is not to be found in this sorrowful world."

" Good is your talk," said the Lord, " but you are only seeking to deceive me, you are in no want of the price of a lodging or of anything to eat, you have gold and silver in your pocket, and you ought to give thanks to God for your having enough to do you till [next] day."

The blind man did not know that it was our Saviour who was talking to him, and he said to him, " It is not sermons but alms I'm asking for, I am certain that if you did know that there was gold or silver about me you would take it from me. Get off now, I don't want your talk."

" Indeed you are a senseless man," said the Lord, " you will not have gold or silver long," and with that He left him.

St. Peter was listening to the discourse, and he had a wish to tell the blind man that it was our Saviour who was talking to him, but he got no opportunity. But there was another man listening when our Saviour said that the blind man had gold and silver. It was a wicked plunderer who was in it, but he knew that our Saviour never told a lie. As soon as He and St. Peter were gone, the robber came to the blind man and said to him, " give me your gold and silver or I'll put a knife through your heart."

" I have no gold or silver," said the blind man, " if I had, I wouldn't be looking for alms." But, with that, the robber caught hold of him, put him under him, and took from him all he had. The blind man shouted and screamed as loud as he was able, and our Saviour and Peter heard him.

" There's wrong being done to the blind man," said Peter.

" Get treacherously and it will go the same way," said our Saviour, " not to speak of the Day of Judgment."

"I understand you, there is nothing hid from you, Master," said Peter.

The day after that they were journeying by a desert, and a greedy lion came out. "Now, Peter," said our Saviour, "you often said that you would lose your life for me, go now and give yourself to the lion, and I shall escape safe."

Peter thought to himself and said, "I would sooner meet any other death than let a lion eat me; we are swift-footed, and we can run from him, but if I see him coming up with us I'll remain behind, and you can escape safe."

"Let it be so," said our Saviour.

The lion gave a roar, and off and away with him after them, and it was not long till he was gaining on them and close up to them.

"Remain behind, Peter," said our Saviour, but Peter let on that he never heard a word, and went running out before his Master. The Lord turned round and said to the lion, "go back to the desert," and so he did.

Peter looked behind him, and when he saw the lion going back, he stood till our Saviour came up with him.

"Peter," said He, "you left me in danger, and—what was worse than that—you told lies."

"I did that," said Peter, "because I knew that you have power over everything, not alone over the lion of the wilderness."

"Silence your mouth, and do not be telling lies; you did *not* know, and if you were to see me in danger to-morrow you would forsake me again. I know the thoughts of your heart."

"I never thought that you did anything that was not right," said Peter.

"That is another lie," said our Saviour. "Do you not

remember the day that I gave alms to the musician who was half drunk, there was wonder on you, and you said to yourself that many's the poor man in great want, whom I refused, and yet that I gave alms to a drunken man because I liked music. The day after that I refused the old friar, and you said that that was not right; and the same evening you remember what happened about the blind man. I will explain to you now why I acted like that. That musician did more good than twenty friars of his sort since ever they were born. He saved a girl's soul from the pains of hell. She wanted a piece of money, and was going to commit a deadly sin to get it, but the musician prevented her and gave her the piece of money, though he himself was in want of a drink at the same time. As for the friar, he was not in want at all; although he had the name of friar he was a limb of the devil, and that was why I paid him no heed. As for the blind man, his God was in his pocket, for the old word is true, ' where your store is your heart will be with it.' "

A short time after that Peter said, " Master, you have a knowledge of the most lonesome thoughts in the heart of man, and from this moment out I submit to you in everything."

About a week after that they were travelling through hills and mountains, and they lost their way. With the fall of the night there came lightning, thunder, and heavy rain. The night was so dark they could not see a sheep's path. Peter fell against a rock and hurt his foot so badly that he was not able to walk a step.

Our Saviour saw a little light under the foot of a hill, and he said to Peter, " remain where you are, and I will go for help to carry you."

" There is no help to be found in this wild place," said Peter, " and don't leave me here in danger by myself."

" Be it so," said our Saviour, and with that he gave a whistle, and there came four men ; and who was captain of them but the person who robbed the blind man a while before that ! He recognized our Saviour and Peter, and told his men to carry Peter carefully to the dwelling-place they had among the hills. " These two put gold and silver in my way a short time ago," said he.

They carried Peter into a chamber under the ground. There was a fine fire in it, and they put the wounded man near it, and gave him a drink. He fell asleep, and our Saviour made the sign of the cross with his finger above the wound, and when he awoke he was able to walk as well as ever. There was wonder on him when he awoke, and he asked " what happened to him." Our Saviour told him each thing and how it occurred.

" I thought," said Peter, " that I was dead, and that I was up at the gate of heaven, but I could not get in, for the door was shut, and there was no doorkeeper to be found."

" It was a vision you had," said our Saviour, " but it is true. Heaven is shut and is not to be opened until I die for the sin of the human race who put anger on My Father. It is not a common but a shameful death I shall get, but I shall rise again gloriously and open the heaven that was shut, and you shall be doorkeeper."

" Ora ! Master," said Peter, " it cannot be that you would get a shameful death. Would you not allow me to die for you ? I am ready and willing."

" You think that," said our Saviour.

The time came when our Saviour was to get death. The evening before that He Himself and His twelve disciples were at supper, when He said, " There is a man of you going to betray Me." There was great trouble on them, and each one of them said, " Am I he ? " But He said, " He who dips with his hand in the dish with Me, he is the man who shall betray Me."

Peter said then, " If the whole world were against you," said he, " I will not be against you." But our Saviour said to him, " Before the cock crows to-night you will reneague (deny) Me three times."

" I would die before I would reneague you," said Peter ; " indeed I shall not reneague you."

When death-judgment was passed upon our Saviour, His enemies were beating Him and spitting on Him. Peter was outside in the court, when there came a servant-girl to him and said to him, " You were with Jesus." " I don't know," says Peter, " what you are saying."

Then when he was going out the gate another girl said, " There's a man who was with Jesus," but he took his oath that he had no knowledge at all of Him. Then some of the people who were listening said, " There is no doubt at all but you were with Him ; we know it by your talk." He took the great oaths, then, that he was not with Him. And on the spot the cock crew, and then he remembered the words our Saviour said, and he wept the tears of repentance, and he found forgiveness from Him whom he denied. He has the keys of heaven now, and if we shed the tears of repentance for our faults, as he shed them, we shall find forgiveness as he found it, and he will welcome us with a hundred thousand welcomes when we go to the door of heaven.

# MARY'S WELL

Long ago there was a blessed well in Ballintubber (*i.e.*, town of the well), in the county Mayo. There was once a monastery in the place where the well is now, and it was on the spot where stood the altar of the monastery that the well broke out. The monastery was on the side of a hill, but when Cromwell and his band of destroyers came to this country, they overthrew the monastery, and never left stone on top of stone in the altar that they did not throw down.

A year from the day that they threw down the altar—that was Lady Day in spring—the well broke out on the site of the altar, and it is a wonderful thing to say, that there was not one drop of water in the stream that was at the foot of the hill from the day that the well broke out.

There was a poor friar going the road the same day, and he went out of his way to say a prayer upon the site of the blessed altar, and there was great wonder on him when he saw a fine well in its place. He fell on his knees and began to say his paternoster, when he heard a voice saying: "Put off your brogues, you are upon blessed ground, you are on the brink of Mary's Well, and there is the curing of thousands of blind in it; there shall be a person cured by the water of that well for every person who heard mass in front of the altar that was in the place where the well is now, if they be dipped three times in it, in the name of the Father, the Son, and the Holy Spirit."

When the friar had his prayers said, he looked up and saw a large white dove upon a fir tree near him. It was the dove who was speaking. The friar was dressed in false clothes, because there was a price on his head, as great as would be on the head of a wild-dog [wolf].

At any rate, he proclaimed the story to the people of the little village, and it was not long till it went out through the country. It was a poor place, and the people in it had nothing [to live in] but huts, and these filled with smoke. On that account there were a great many weak-eyed people amongst them. With the dawn, on the next day, there were above forty people at Mary's Well, and there was never man nor woman of them but came back with good sight.

The fame of Mary's Well went through the country, and it was not long till there were pilgrims from every county coming to it, and nobody went back without being cured; and at the end of a little time even people from other countries used to be coming to it.

There was an unbeliever living near Mary's Well. It was a gentleman he was, and he did not believe in the cure. He said there was nothing in it but pishtrogues (charms), and to make a mock of the people he brought a blind ass, that he had, to the well, and he dipped its head under the water. The ass got its sight, but the scoffer was brought home as blind as the sole of your shoe.

At the end of a year it so happened that there was a priest working as a gardener with the gentleman who was blind. The priest was dressed like a workman, and nobody at all knew that it was a priest who was in it. One day the gentleman was sickly, and he asked his servant to take him out into the garden. When he came to the place where the priest was working he sat down. " Isn't it a great pity," says he, " that I cannot see my fine garden ? "

The gardener took compassion on him, and said, " I

know where there is a man who would cure you, but there is a price on his head on account of his religion."

"I give my word that I'll do no spying on him, and I'll pay him well for his trouble," said the gentleman.

"But perhaps you would not like to go through the mode of curing that he has," says the gardener.

"I don't care what mode he has, if he gives me my sight," said the gentleman.

Now, the gentleman had an evil character, because he betrayed a number of priests before that. Bingham was the name that was on him. However, the priest took courage and said, "Let your coach be ready on to-morrow morning, and I will drive you to the place of the cure; neither coachman nor anyone else may be present but myself, and do not tell to anyone at all where you are going, or give anyone a knowledge of what is your business."

On the morning of the next day Bingham's coach was ready, and he himself got into it, with the gardener driving him. "Do you remain at home this time," says he to the coachman, "and the gardener will drive me." The coachman was a villain, and there was jealousy on him. He conceived the idea of watching the coach to see what way they were to go. His blessed vestments were on the priest, inside of his other clothes. When they came to Mary's Well the priest said to him, "I am going to get back your sight for you in the place where you lost it." Then he dipped him three times in the well, in the name of the Father, the Son, and the Holy Spirit, and his sight came to him as well as ever it was.

"I'll give you a hundred pounds," said Bingham, "as soon as I go home."

The coachman was watching, and as soon as he saw the priest in his blessed vestments, he went to the people of the law, and betrayed the priest. He was taken and hanged, without judge, without judgment. The man who was after getting back his sight could have saved the priest, but he did not speak a word in his behalf.

About a month after this another priest came to Bingham, and he dressed like a gardener, and he asked work of Bingham, and got it from him; but he was not long in his service until an evil thing happened to Bingham. He went out one day walking through his fields, and there met him a good-looking girl, the daughter of a poor man, and he assaulted her and left her half dead. The girl had three brothers, and they took an oath that they would kill him as soon as they could get hold of him. They had not long to wait. They caught him in the same place where he assaulted the girl, and hanged him on a tree, and left him there hanging.

On the morning of the next day millions of flies were gathered like a great hill round about the tree, and nobody could go near it on account of the foul smell that was round the place, and anyone who would go near it the midges would blind them.

Bingham's wife and son offered a hundred pounds to anyone who would bring out the body. A good many people made an effort to do that, but they were not able. They got dust to shake on the flies, and boughs of trees to beat them with, but they were not able to scatter them, nor to go as far as the tree. The foul smell was getting worse, and the neighbours were afraid that the flies and noisome corpse would bring a plague upon them.

The second priest was at this time a gardener with Bingham, but the people of the house did not know that it was a priest who was in it, for if the people of the law or the spies knew, they would take and hang him. The Catholics went to Bingham's wife and told her that they knew a man who would banish the flies. "Bring him to me," said she, "and if he is able to banish the flies, that is not the reward he'll get, but seven times as much."

"But," said they, "if the people of the law knew, they would take him and hang him, as they hung the man who got back the sight of his eyes for him before." "But," said she, "could not he banish the flies without the knowledge of the people of the law?"

"We don't know," said they, "until we take counsel with him."

That night they took counsel with the priest and told him what Bingham's wife said.

"I have only an earthly life to lose," said the priest, "and I shall give it up for the sake of the poor people, for there will be a plague in the country unless I banish the flies. On to-morrow morning I shall make an attempt to banish them in the name of God, and I have hope and confidence in God that he will save me from my enemies. Go to the lady now, and tell her that I shall be near the tree at sunrise to-morrow morning, and tell her to have men ready to put the corpse in the grave."

They went to the lady and told her all the priest said.

"If it succeeds with him," said she, "I shall have the reward ready for him, and I shall order seven men to be present."

The priest spent that night in prayer, and half an hour before sunrise he went to the place where his blessed vestments were hidden; he put these on, and with a cross in one hand, and with holy-water in the other, he went to the place where were the flies. He then began reading out of his book and scattering holy-water on the flies, in the name of the Father, the Son, and the Holy Ghost. The hill of flies rose, and flew up into the air, and made the heaven as dark as night. The people did not know where they went, but at the end of half an hour there was not one of them to be seen

There was great joy on the people, but it was not long till they saw the spy coming, and they called to the priest to run away as quick as it was in him to run. The priest gave to the butts (took to his heels), and the spy followed him, and a knife in each hand with him. When he was not able to come up with the priest he flung the knife after him. As the knife was flying out past the priest's shoulder he put up his left hand and caught it, and without ever looking behind him he flung it back. It struck the man and went through his heart, so that he fell dead and the priest went free.

The people got the body of Bingham and buried it in the grave, but when they went to bury the body of the spy they found thousands of rats round about it, and there was not a morsel of flesh on his bones that they had not eaten. They would not stir from the body, and the people were not able to rout them away, so that they had to leave the bones over-ground.

The priest hid away his blessed vestments and was working in the garden when Bingham's wife sent for him, and told him to take the reward that was for banishing the flies, and to give it to the man who banished them, if he knew him.

" I do know him, and he told me to bring him the reward to-night, because he has the intention of leaving the country before the law-people hang him."

" Here it is for you," said she, as she handed him a purse of gold.

On the morning of the next day the priest went to the brink of the sea, and found a ship that was going to France. He went on board, and as soon as he had left the harbour he put his priest's-clothes on him, and gave thanks to God for bringing him safe. We do not know what happened to him from that out.

After that, blind and sore-eyed people used to be coming to Mary's Well, and not a person of them ever returned without being cured. But there never yet was anything good in this country that was not spoilt by somebody, and the well was spoilt in this way.

There was a girl in Ballintubber and she was about to be married, when there came a half-blind old woman to her asking alms in the honour of God and Mary.

" I've nothing to give to an old blind-thing of a hag, it's bothered with them I am," said the girl.

" That the marriage ring may never go on you until you're as blind as myself," says the old woman.

Next day, in the morning, the young girl's eyes were sore, and the morning after that she was nearly blind, and the neighbours said to her that she ought to go to Mary's Well.

In the morning, early, she rose up and went to the well, but what should she see at it but the old woman who asked the alms of her, sitting on the brink, combing her head over the blessed well.

" Destruction on you, you nasty hag, is it dirtying Mary's Well you are ? " said the girl. " Get out of that or I'll break your neck."

" You have no honour nor regard for God or Mary, you refused to give alms in honour of them, and for that reason you shall not dip yourself in the well."

The girl caught a hold of the hag trying to pull her from the well, and with the dragging that was between them, the two of them fell into the well and were drowned.

From that day to this there has been no cure in the well.

DATE DUE